MW01206404

Amelia Bloomer: From Petticoats to Politics

MARKO D

ISBN:9798862378184

Table of Contents

Acknowledgments

Recognizing those who've influenced us goes beyond mere politeness; it's an homage to the intricate blend of experiences, mentors, and relationships that define our identity. When considering Amelia Bloomer's life, it's tempting to envision her as a lone revolutionary battling the staid traditions of her time. But even icons don't stand alone; they are often bolstered by a network of supporters, influencers, and even critics who help define their journey. Would Amelia be Amelia without these figures who both challenged and championed her?

Take Elizabeth Cady Stanton, for instance. What does it mean for two like-minded activists to collide in the cauldron of social reform? Their friendship wasn't just a meeting of minds but a fusion of ambitions. Stanton pushed Amelia to question the status quo, not just adapt to it. It was a pivotal friendship, each influencing the other to challenge the societal norms that shackled women. When you think of one, it's hard not to ponder the other.

And then, there was Dexter Bloomer — the husband who was not just a spouse but a partner in every sense. While it's common now to speak of equitable marriages, the idea was revolutionary during Amelia's time. Dexter's unwavering support, both emotionally and editorially, wasn't just significant; it was transformative. How many other women of Amelia's era had partners who tolerated and actively supported their public endeavours? Through consistent backing, Dexter shaped Amelia's journey and modelled a different marriage for the public.

We must also tip our hats to the critics and detractors. Yes, you read that correctly. While it might be unorthodox to thank one's critics, consider this: Opposition has a way of sharpening our arguments, forcing us to reevaluate and, if needed, bolster our viewpoints. Every sarcastic column and dismissive article that mocked Amelia's bloomers or her ambitions only deepened her resolve. They became the grit in the oyster, unwittingly contributing to the creation of the pearl that was Amelia's legacy. Who are we without our struggles?

Last but not least, let us acknowledge the readers of Amelia's time and, by extension, you — the modern-day reader. Amelia wrote to express herself, connect influence, and inspire action. A writer writes, yes, but the reader completes the narrative, takes the ideas presented and decides what to do with them.

So, as we delve into the life of Amelia Bloomer, let's remember this interconnected web of individuals who played a part, however large or small, in shaping this incredible woman. Just as Amelia stood on the shoulders of giants, so did we all. And in recognizing them, we understand not just Amelia but also the complex, beautiful intricacy of human life.

The Enigma of Amelia Bloomer

Who was Amelia Bloomer? It's a question that is simple in its asking but complex in its answering. This 19th-century icon challenges our modern-day assumptions at every turn, becoming, in the process, a riddle wrapped in the garb of her time. And ah, that garb — the famous "Bloomers" that we might hastily, but incorrectly, credit her with inventing. How can one woman be at once a social reformer, a journalist, and a fashion revolutionary?

Picture her beginnings in Homer, New York, a town that wasn't exactly teeming with opportunities for ambitious women. Imagine being Amelia in such a place. Does the environment make the person, or does the person challenge their environment? As we go on, you'll see how this tight-knit community shaped Amelia and was irrevocably altered by her disruptive presence.

Those iconic "Bloomers?" Let's clarify: Amelia didn't craft the first pair with her hands. But the way she embraced them, they might have been her creation. What did they symbolize for her? Not just fabric and stitches but a call to arms. These garments were an emblem of a life unrestricted, a challenge to the sartorial and social confines women found themselves in.

Move on to "The Lily," her famed newspaper. Initially, a modest journal focusing on temperance, Amelia transformed it into a roaring megaphone for the cries of women's suffrage and societal reform. How did she juggle these multiple roles, negotiating the delicate balance between societal norms and radical activism? Our story will take you behind her editor's desk, revealing the woman who gave voice to the voiceless.

And what about Dexter Bloomer, her life partner? Dexter wasn't just the supporting actor in Amelia's play; he was a co-director. At a time when marriage could be a woman's creative end, Amelia and Dexter's union was something of a marvel — an egalitarian partnership. How did two people in the 19th century manage a modern marriage based on mutual respect and shared dreams?

Here's the essence: Amelia Bloomer isn't merely a woman who stood up against her time. She's a prism through which we can view the multifaceted battles she chose and those who chose her. We'll wade through her highs and lows, explore her personal relationships, and inspect her public stances. Doing so can unravel the tangled web of her life's work and influence.

Amelia had both her champions and her critics. Some hailed her as a visionary, while others dismissed her as a fleeting sensation or a societal menace. How did Amelia walk this thin line between praise and disdain? Her steadfast nature wasn't just a mark of stubbornness but a sign of her utter conviction in the need for change.

And let's not forget Amelia was a living, breathing human with private joys and sorrows. Was Amelia at the family table the same woman who penned passionate editorials in "The Lily"? We'll delve into how her private life and public persona danced in complex harmony, each influencing the other subtly yet profoundly.

Is Amelia Bloomer's story just a historical curiosity or a living testament? Does she belong in the past, or does her story continue to echo in our contemporary struggles? As you'll see, the answer is always complex, but the journey to find it is worth taking.

So, are you ready to jump into the depths of Amelia Bloomer's life? Ready to unravel the puzzle that she poses? As we turn the page to the next chapter, remember that Amelia Bloomer isn't just a historical figure to be analyzed. She's a challenge, an enigma, and an everlasting symbol of what can happen when one person asks, "Why not?" Let's embark on this journey together; Amelia Bloomer is a mystery too captivating to be left unsolved.

Chapter 1

Early Whispers of Change

Imagine a young girl growing up in Cortland County, New York, during the early 19th century. For most, this conjures up images of pastoral landscapes, close-knit communities, and a life confined mainly to domestic spheres. This was the backdrop against which Amelia Bloomer's life began — serene, predictable, and yet brimming with inconsistencies that Amelia would spend a lifetime challenging.

Ah, Cortland County. A place where rolling hills met the confined aspirations of women and where men's dreams extended as far as the horizon. What could lead Amelia to rise above her circumstances, born into a society that offered her a predestined, almost stifling future? A simple question with a profound answer: unquenchable curiosity.

Amelia was no ordinary girl. Born Amelia Jenks in 1818, she was raised in a family that didn't possess immense wealth or social standing. The Jenks family offered Amelia what they could, but it was a little regarding material wealth. Despite these restrictions, or perhaps because of them, Amelia exhibited a robust intellect and a tenacity for questioning conventional wisdom. Even in her early years, you could see a revolutionary spark igniting in her eyes — a spark that refused to be dimmed by the societal norms of her time.

Was she a prodigy? Not exactly. Amelia was, however, an anomaly in a world that preferred its women to be neither seen nor intellectually present. This wasn't an era that took kindly to a woman with a book in one hand and a sceptical frown directed at gender norms. The Cortland community found it hard to label Amelia. Too spirited to be just a housewife, yet too feminine to reject the domestic role altogether. Society, with its strict bifurcations, was confounded by Amelia.

Her youthful days in Cortland served as the kindling for her future activism. As a young woman, she was interested in the moral reform movements sweeping the United States. Moral reform, in this era, was not merely a buzzword; it was the epicentre of social consciousness, touching on temperance, suffrage, and education reform. For Amelia, these were not merely issues to be debated by men in smoky taverns; these were the very ropes that tied women to the mast of social confinement.

And let's not underestimate the importance of the social circles Amelia frequented. Her early friends and acquaintances were not just a gathering of minds; they were her sounding board, the crucible in which her views were tested, strengthened, and, at times, vehemently opposed. Contrary to popular belief, strong convictions don't emerge from a vacuum. They are often forged in the crucible of lively intellectual exchanges. Amelia sought that as voraciously as she did the books she read.

Amelia's young life was a whirlwind of intellectual exploration layered with a growing awareness of the social injustices around her. Her blossoming consciousness was not just confined to books or secret conversations with like-minded women. Amelia was awakening to the gender imbalance in society, and she couldn't unsee it, no matter how much the world around her tried to draw the curtains.

In her late teens, she made a move that would prove pivotal to her activism — she became a schoolteacher. This was no small feat for a woman during a time when education was mainly the domain of men. Amelia Jenks, who would later become Amelia Bloomer, took a decisive step into education to make ends meet and shape minds — young minds that could rise above the confines of Cortland County and 19th-century America.

Let's pause here for a moment and take this in. Looking at Amelia's life retrospectively, we might think it was a foregone conclusion that she would shake the social fabric of her time. But remember, each choice Amelia made was a calculated risk. With every book read, every class taught, and every norm questioned, Amelia laid the foundation for an unpredictable but groundbreaking future.

If Cortland County thought it had seen the last of Amelia's rebellious ways, it needed to be corrected. These were but the early whispers of change, the stirrings of a revolution that would echo through the annals of American history. This chapter was merely a prologue to a life that would challenge, confront, and ultimately redefine the social fabric of a nation. How was Cortland County, how was America, to know that this young woman would bloom into a figure who would redefine the meaning of womanhood in America?

So, in this nurturing yet confining soil of Cortland County, Amelia Bloomer took root. Yet even as she grew in this familiar terrain, the young Amelia Jenks began stretching her branches towards the sky, her leaves catching whispers of change. These whispers would one day turn into roars, and the world had yet to hear Amelia Bloomer's full voice. And what a voice it would be.

Childhood in Cortland County

Ah, the hills and dales of Cortland County, New York — bucolic scenes where norms rather than dreams usually scripted childhoods. Picture the tranquillity, the crisp air, and the quaint villages that dotted the landscape in the early 1800s. Now, drop Amelia Jenks into this setting. What emerges isn't a portrait of pastoral simplicity but a vivid tableau humming with potential and divergence.

Born in 1818, Amelia arrived when the ink was already dry on the role that society had scripted for women. The vision of women's future was as confined as the corsets they wore. And Amelia? She first encountered the rigidity of this societal mould during her formative years in Cortland County. The norms of Cortland County served as the crucible for Amelia's activism. The more society tried to contain her, the more her innate resistance pushed back. It's not far-fetched that Cortland County inadvertently created its own subversive.

The Jenks family was neither wealthy nor socially prominent. They were humble farmers. Amelia's childhood was not one of privilege or extravagant educational opportunities. This era did not offer women — especially those of limited means — access to formal education. However, Amelia's intellectual ambitions simmered beneath the surface, taking root in the farmland soil that her family tilled. Was it the confinement of her environment that sharpened her intellect, or was it her intellect that refused to be confined? It's akin to the age-old question about the chicken and the egg — one can't pinpoint where it began, but the impact was undeniable.

When young Amelia went to the village schools, which she did with an eagerness that outstripped many of her peers, she found education both a liberator and a captor. While books offered windows into new worlds, they also inadvertently reinforced gender stereotypes. Schooling in the 19th century was less about cultivating the mind and more about preparing for predetermined societal roles. Young girls like Amelia were expected to emerge as virtuous wives and mothers rather than independent thinkers. Yet, Amelia's youthful academic pursuits were not merely exercises in rote memorization; they were acts of subtle rebellion. Every book she read, every lesson she questioned, was a chip in the tower of the social norms that were supposed to contain her.

You might wonder — what fuels a young girl's determination to break the moulds set before her? The answer lies in an uncanny blend of intellectual curiosity and social circumstance. Amelia didn't merely digest what she learned; she interrogated it. Perhaps her first steps towards activism were not grand public statements but silent questions she posed to her teachers, textbooks, and, most importantly, herself. Amelia was coming of age in a period rife with social and moral reform movements — abolitionism, temperance, and religious revivals — and these seismic shifts didn't go unnoticed by her.

It's crucial to consider the company Amelia kept during her childhood. While still a girl, she had the uncanny ability to attract like-minded individuals. Her friends were her first audience, critics, and earliest allies. These friendships were not merely social engagements but revolutionary councils in disguise. With her friends, Amelia began to articulate her discontent with society's prescriptions. Through these relationships, Amelia found the audacity to challenge the very structure of the world she was born into.

It's hard to underestimate the grit it takes to question established norms, especially for a young girl in early 19th-century America. Amelia's resilience did not exist in a vacuum; it was the product of her environment, family, education, and character. Each hardship she faced consolidated her commitment to reform; each opposition made her more persistent.

So, there we have Amelia Jenks, a young girl raised in Cortland County, forming her worldview amidst societal limitations and personal ambitions. As she navigated the roles imposed upon her by her community, Amelia became increasingly aware that these were roles she was unwilling to play. She wasn't rebellious for the sake of being defiant; she was rebellious because obedience would have meant the suppression of her very essence.

Before she could ever contemplate challenging the suffocating norms of the wider world, Amelia had to confront the limitations within her microcosm—her family, her school, and her community. In that small world, she laid the foundation for a life of activism. This life would one day disrupt the status quo far beyond the boundaries of Cortland County. Though seemingly ordinary, her early years were anything but; they were the quiet, transformative period in which Amelia Jenks grew into Amelia Bloomer. And while Cortland County may have been the cocoon, Amelia was always destined to be the butterfly.

An Unusual Girl in a Conventional World

Imagine an era when femininity was boxed within layers of fabric and social etiquette — each stitch, each fold, a metaphor for limitation. That was America in the 1800s. But what happens when a girl doesn't fit the mould? Enter Amelia Jenks Bloomer. Even her name, a harbinger of blossoming things, argued against her confined existence. But let's not get ahead of ourselves; let's travel back to her formative years in Cortland County.

Amelia was not an ordinary girl — not by the standards of her time, nor by today's. Conventionality? It wasn't in her vocabulary. To understand the impact she would later make on society, we must first peer into her childhood and her development in a world that largely dismissed women's intellectual capacity. Amelia could not be caged, neither by words nor by garments. Can you imagine that? A young girl, a prospective wife and mother, daring to question the limits placed on her gender?

But we're not talking about overt rebellion. Amelia's rebellion was in her insatiable curiosity, persistent questioning, and refusal to accept "no" when asking for education for the chance to contribute to conversations other than those about knitting and courtship. This wasn't a sporadic defiance but a continuous, under-the-skin itch for more. Can you sense the audacity in that?

Let's tackle the educational aspect first. As we know, Amelia loved to learn. Most girls of her era were trained to read just enough scripture to maintain purity, but Amelia craved more. She sought books and discussions that fostered a sense of intellectual kinship, particularly gravitating toward religious and moral debates. When other girls her age daydreamed of marriage proposals, Amelia envisioned a society restructured to honour the contributions of both genders. It's no small thing to step out of the educational limitations set for you. How many of us, even today, are courageous enough to question what we're taught?

Amelia understood the power dynamics as she grew, even if she couldn't articulate them. She was an observer not merely of the outward rituals of society but also of the inward moralities that guided them. Where did these morals, often mere justifications for inequities, originate? These weren't mere ponderings; they were the stirrings of a future activist.

And what about love and marriage? These universal aspects of human life were equally trapped within rigid boundaries. Although not impervious to love, Amelia saw marriage as a partnership rather than a form of female containment. She did not shy away from intellectual discourse when she met Dexter

Bloomer, a lawyer and a newspaper editor who matched her intellectual vigour. Most men might have baulked at her audacity. Dexter, however, became her most steadfast supporter.

What could be more non-conforming than that — a woman in the 19th century expecting, no, demanding equality in a marriage? This was a couple united in holy matrimony and a partnership that defied social norms. Amelia didn't become Mrs. Dexter Bloomer; she remained Amelia Bloomer, a distinct, autonomous entity. Do you realize how seismic this was in a world that considered women an extension of their husbands?

Let's turn to Amelia's budding journalistic endeavours. When she took over the editorial helm of "The Lily," she broke yet another barrier. Publishing pieces on temperance was one thing, but when she used the platform to discuss women's issues, she changed the game. A woman using the press to challenge societal norms? Unheard of. Her audacity was a whirlwind sweeping through a forest of staid ideas, uprooting convention wherever it touched down.

And yet, it would be a mistake to paint Amelia as a defiant firebrand without understanding her complexities. Amid her activism, she still embodied specific traditional roles of her time. She was, after all, a wife and a devout Christian, deeply committed to temperance and moral reform. This didn't make her any less subversive; instead, it made her a multi-dimensional human, navigating the ever-changing tides of her individuality and her environment.

There you have it — Amelia Bloomer, a singular entity in a world that wanted to clone her into a caricature of femininity. She was a walking, talking paradox who existed within her era's boundaries even as she spent her life pushing against them. The beauty of Amelia was not just in her resistance but in her willingness to be complex, to be an "unusual girl" in a world of stifling norms. Isn't it fascinating how sometimes the loudest disruptors are those who don't seem to be shouting at all? Amelia was not merely a disruptor; she was an invitation to complexity in a world that sought to simplify her, a question mark in a narrative that wanted to put a period at the end of her sentence. She was, indeed, an unusual girl in a conventional world.

The Sparks of Intellectual Curiosity

Now, let's turn the pages of time and space, focusing on a particular facet of Amelia's life — her boundless intellectual curiosity. Do you remember the first time you questioned the world around you? That sensation of holding an unanswered question, like a riddle begging to be solved? Amelia felt that early in her life; these weren't just passing thoughts for her. They were sparks igniting a lifelong flame.

Education for women in the 1800s was far from what we consider standard today. Yet young Amelia didn't view the restrictive educational standards as the unchangeable status quo; she saw them as challenges to be conquered. Most girls received just enough schooling to read the Bible and manage household accounts. But Amelia? She wanted more. She wanted Shakespeare and Milton, math and history, philosophy and ethics. While many resigned to their 'proper place,' Amelia dreamed of classrooms, podiums, and ink and paper. Who could blame her?

Her quest for knowledge wasn't a quiet one. Amelia sought books beyond the 'approved' reading list for young women. Imagine her in a room, perhaps a corner of her home, engrossed in tomes of philosophy and science, utterly unfazed by society's frowns. The crux here isn't merely her defiance but her audacity to believe that she had the right to those pages and ideas. We talked about "lean in" today; Amelia leaned so far that she practically toppled the table.

In those early years, Dexter Bloomer entered her life. A newspaper editor and lawyer by profession, he was also a man of substantial intellect. At a time when women were expected to listen rather than speak, to nod rather than question, their courtship was far from typical. Can you imagine their conversations, steeped in intellectual rigour, resonating with notions that women had every right to sit at society's table? Dexter didn't just love Amelia; he respected her. And in the 19th century, that was revolutionary.

Soon, the couple relocated to Seneca Falls, New York — a name that will always symbolize women's rights. It was here that Amelia's intellectual pursuits found their true north. Seneca Falls was a hotbed of reformist ideas, and Amelia soaked them in like a sponge submerged in water. How could she not? She was surrounded by like-minded souls, after all. Women and men who believed in change who challenged the norms just as she did. It was the perfect soil for the seeds of her intellectual curiosity to sprout into tangible action finally.

With Dexter's encouragement, Amelia ventured into journalism, becoming the editor of "The Lily," a temperance newspaper that soon transformed under her stewardship. Initially focusing on temperance — a safe topic, if there was one — she found her voice growing more assertive, her topics shifting. "The Lily" metamorphosed from a journal discussing sobriety to questioning the foundation of women's roles. Could a woman, should a woman, have aspirations beyond her home? Amelia not only believed so but used the power of the press to disseminate this radical idea.

But let's remember that Amelia was a woman of balance who could talk about politics and reforms while deeply invested in spirituality and morality. This blend of secular and religious curiosity made her unique. She could simultaneously discuss the Ten Commandments and the Constitution and find the most missed connections. Was it contradictory? To some, perhaps. But Amelia saw no discrepancy between being a devout Christian and a passionate reformist. Why should her faith limit her activism or vice versa?

Her curiosity was not confined to theory; it split into practical life. Remember the Bloomer costume? Those 'scandalous' trousers directly resulted from Amelia questioning the very fabric of women's existence. She questioned the restrictive attire women had to wear — layers of heavy, cumbersome skirts — and publicized an alternative. The costume was practical, allowing women physical freedom they had never known. Practicality, intellect, and courage — in Amelia, these weren't isolated traits but interconnected aspects of a complex personality.

This is Amelia Bloomer — a woman never content with what she was 'supposed to know,' a woman who understood that to question is to live. Can we sum her up? Likely not. She defies easy labels and single-story narratives. Yet if one were to try, you could say she was an intellectual adventurer, always on the brink of a discovery, whether within the pages of a book, the walls of a convention, or the folds of a garment. In her quest for knowledge and unyielding curiosity, Amelia Bloomer reminds us that the questions we ask sometimes shape the world more than the answers

Chapter 2

The Awakening

Picture this: Amelia, a young woman now, living in a world heavy with norms and conventions. She understands what society expects from her — marriage, children, and a comfortable domesticity. That should be enough, shouldn't it? For most, perhaps, but not for Amelia Bloomer. Her life was destined to be a tapestry of the unconventional. But how did she awaken to her uncommon path?

Life unfolded in Seneca Falls, New York, where the winds carried whispers of change. Dexter, her husband, ran a local newspaper called "The Seneca County Courier," Amelia would often assist him in editing and correspondence. But assisting wasn't enough — she was a woman with a thousand questions and ideas. The room that once felt like an extension of her passion was shrinking around her, a cage veiling her capabilities. So what does a woman do when the room isn't large enough to contain her ambition?

In her case, Amelia found an alternative space to flourish — "The Lily." Initially intended as a temperance journal for women, Amelia took the helm and, in doing so, moulded it into something more — a mouthpiece for women's rights. When the ink from her pen touched the paper, it wasn't just an imprint; it was a pledge, an act of defiance against a society that wanted women to be seen and not heard. And hear her, they did. "The Lily" became a platform that went beyond temperance, venturing into controversial issues like voting and property rights. But what drove Amelia to turn "The Lily" into such an unexpected voice?

This transformative period wasn't just the result of an intellectual epiphany. No, it was born from encounters with other towering figures of the time, notably Elizabeth Cady Stanton and Susan B. Anthony. Remember, these women were giants, each with her ideas and will to ignite change. But rather than overshadow Amelia, their towering presence seemed to pull her upward. Stanton, with her unparalleled eloquence, and Anthony, with her vibrant activism, stirred something within Amelia, adding fuel to the sparks of her intellectual curiosity. So, if you wonder whether the individual or the environment shaped her, consider this: it was a symphony of both.

While her editorial pursuits were vital, Amelia's public presence also began to grow. Could she merely sit behind a desk, knowing that her voice could resonate within the walls of town halls and open spaces? The answer was a resounding no. She took her beliefs to the streets and the podiums. Women's rights conventions became her stage, and Amelia, a performer, captivated her audience with her convictions' authenticity. Think of it — each word she spoke in public was a stone thrown into the stagnant pond of patriarchy, creating ripples that reached far and wide.

Yet the blossoming of Amelia wasn't confined to what she said or wrote. It translated into how she presented herself. It was in the audacity of trousers, of the 'Bloomer costume,' named in her honour, that Amelia made one of her most memorable stands. Why trousers, you ask? Because in a world that sought to restrict her, she understood the power of freedom, even if that freedom started with something as essential as the clothes one wears. The "Bloomer costume" wasn't a fashion statement but a political act. Trousers may seem inconsequential today, but they were nothing short of revolutionary back then.

Amelia's activism wasn't about bragging; it was rooted in the minutiae of daily life. She realized that empowerment began at home, in the privacy of one's thoughts, clothes, and words one writes. Her awakening was an intricate weave of intellectual pursuit and tangible action. This symbiotic relationship made her neither an armchair philosopher nor a mindless activist.

And so, during a tumultuous era, Amelia Bloomer emerged as more than a character in the annals of history. She became an embodiment of an idea: that the private can be political, that the minute can be monumental, and that a single voice can echo through the corridors of change. This was her awakening, the crossing of a personal Rubicon, an audacious foray into territories deemed forbidden for women.

How do we encapsulate such a transformation? Perhaps we don't. Let Amelia be the complex, multi-dimensional figure she was. After all, isn't it fitting that a woman who refused to fit the mould remains unfixed, fluid in our collective memory? Indeed, in her awakening, Amelia Bloomer teaches us that some things — some people — are too expansive to be contained. And so, they shouldn't be.

First Marriage: The Match That Wasn't

Ah, matrimony! That institution is often hailed as the cornerstone of a woman's life. But what happens when the cornerstones are uneven? When Amelia Jenks married Dexter Bloomer in 1840, society applauded, but should they have? After all, Dexter was a good catch — a man of intellect and ambition, a newspaper editor. He wasn't just any man but a progressive man who respected Amelia's intellect. Yet, this story isn't so straightforward.

Dexter's paper, "The Seneca County Courier," operated out of Seneca Falls, New York, which would host the historic Women's Rights Convention in 1848. This environment was fertile ground for the seeds of Amelia's political awakening. But before that, it was also the backdrop for a marriage that, in some respects, wasn't quite the idyllic match society would have us believe.

It's one thing to marry a man who respects your intelligence. It's another to marry a man who understands your ambition. Dexter was no ogre, but let's be clear: the 1840s didn't groom men to value their wives as intellectual equals or social activists. Even the most enlightened men had blind spots. In the household, traditional roles persisted. Amelia was expected to be — first and foremost — a homemaker and a wife. To that end, she was exemplary, managing the household while her husband managed his newspaper. But the home became a cage, a constraint on Amelia's intellectual appetite.

So why did she marry him in the first place? Was it love? Convenience? Social pressure? Likely a mixture, as it often is. But whatever her reason, her marriage was a testament to the complexities of human relationships. Amelia and Dexter's union wasn't a tragic mismatch or an unqualified success. Amelia, with her burgeoning sense of social justice, and Dexter, a man whose business thrived on the societal norms his wife would come to question — they existed in a paradox.

But here's the marvel: The marriage didn't suffocate Amelia; it propelled her. Dexter's newspaper was her doorway into the world of journalism. The tools of his trade became the tools of her emancipation. Could the inadequacies of her marriage be precisely what fueled her urge to reach beyond it? If so, this match that wasn't a match became the crucible for Amelia's transformation.

Think about it — how many people have taken the oppressive circumstances of their lives and turned them into a launching pad? Amelia did just that. While she began by writing for Dexter's paper, she would later create her own — "The Lily." It was a publication focused initially on temperance. Eventually, it blossomed into an organ for women's liberation, spreading its petals wide to include issues like voting and property rights for women. In this publication, Amelia found her authentic voice. This voice reverberated far beyond the four walls of her marital home.

You might argue that Dexter deserves some credit. After all, didn't he introduce Amelia to the world of publishing? Yes, but it's crucial to recognize that Dexter's role was a catalyst, not a creator. He provided the space, but Amelia filled it with her substance, stretching it, testing its limits until it could hold no more, and she had to build a room.

The layers of their marriage are many, each revealing a different shade of compromise and growth, limitation and transcendence. In many ways, their union mirrors the broader complexities of the time — an era struggling with its mismatched ideals and harsh realities.

In dissecting Amelia's first marriage, we confront an inconvenient truth: Sometimes, it's not the perfect matches that shape us but the imperfect ones. These unions force us to confront our contradictions, stretch the boundaries of what we thought possible, and grow in unexpected directions. Such was the marriage of Amelia and Dexter Bloomer — not a fairy tale but a chapter in a life rich with complexities, one that set the stage for the remarkable woman Amelia would become.

This is more than just a tale of marital discord or harmony. This is the story of how a woman, constrained by her time and circumstances, took what could have been a life sentence and turned it into a life story. What could be more audacious — and inspiring — than that?

Finding Her Voice: The Early Years

Ah, the early years! That formative time when life seemed more like a blank canvas than a structured path. When Amelia Jenks was born in 1818 in Homer, New York, who could've known that this baby girl, swathed in layers of expectation even as a newborn, would grow up to be a woman who would redefine the layers women could wear—literally and metaphorically? What mechanisms shape us during these early years, and how do they carve out the space for a voice as distinct as Amelia's?

Amelia's background was modest, but that word hardly captures the texture of her early life. Born to Ananias and Lucy Webb Jenks, she was one of several children in a family that hovered precariously on the ledge of genteel poverty. While we often romanticize humble beginnings, let's not gloss over the grim reality: economic limitations can muzzle the boldest voices. But, in Amelia's case, her upbringing provided an unplanned advantage. Deprivation prompted resourcefulness; scarcity cultivated resilience. These aren't mere clichés but tangible qualities that Amelia would later channel into her activism.

Growing up in a family with limited resources, Amelia Jenks received only a sparse formal education, a situation common for women of her time. What makes a young girl take a sceptical glance at the boundaries drawn around her and decide to push? For Amelia, it was the natural curiosity inherited from her parents. Her father, a veteran of the Revolutionary War, was an independent man, and her mother a woman of determination. They might not have been scholars, but they knew the value of a good question. And good questions, let's face it, are the primordial soup from which great thinkers evolve.

Books were Amelia's early sanctuaries, her windows to worlds beyond the narrow horizons of Homer. For a voracious young reader, books weren't just an escape but a dialogue. How often do we underestimate the power of literature to challenge, question, and introduce us to unsettling ideas and unfamiliar people? Amelia read not only to affirm her beliefs but to confront them, to engage with words as if they were living entities. This intellectual communion—enabling her to explore the realms of philosophy, history, and social theories—provided her with the tools she would later need in her activist life.

Here's the curious part. While reading was Amelia's doorway to broader intellectual pursuits, the tactile craft of teaching first offered her a platform to articulate her evolving ideas. At the age of 22, Amelia commenced her teaching career. A schoolroom, you see, is both a battleground and a training ground. In teaching children, Amelia was also teaching herself, honing her skills in persuasion, organization, and rhetoric.

As we've previously explored, it wasn't long before she met Dexter Bloomer — a man who would be a significant figure in her life, for better or worse. Dexter introduced her to another form of expression—journalism. Think about it: How did a young woman in her 20s in the 19th century break into a field like journalism without a college education or family connections? It wasn't just luck. It was tenacity and a voice that refused to be silenced.

So, we arrive at a point of reflection. Suppose we rewind the tape of Amelia's early life. In that case, we notice how a lack of formal education and economic resources were, paradoxically, her allies. These supposed 'deficiencies' didn't throttle her voice; they modulated it and gave it a unique timbre. Sometimes, you make your path when you need a paved road.

In tracing Amelia's journey from the unschooled girl in Homer to a young woman making her first mark in Seneca Falls, we witness the alchemy of character. It's the transformation of raw elements—economic constraints, limited formal education, societal norms—into something precious: a voice that not only reverberated through the chambers of her immediate community but would echo through the annals of history.

Why do some voices find their melody so early while others take years? There's no easy answer, but in Amelia Bloomer's case, perhaps it was a perfect storm: A challenging environment met with a formidable spirit, creating a storm that would sweep away the cobwebs of conventionality. And thus, Amelia began her lifelong journey, her voice gradually climbing in octaves, reaching a pitch that could shatter glass ceilings. If you listened closely, you could already hear the reverberations in those early years, a prelude to the powerful symphony her life would become.

Chapter 3

A Bloomer in Bloom

How does a young woman, born to an economically precarious life in Homer, New York, find herself redefining womanhood for an entire generation? We've seen Amelia's formative years, her early engagement with the written word, and the nurturing of a questioning mind. Now, we stand on the threshold of a crucial phase in her life: the period where Amelia transforms into Amelia Bloomer — an activist, a journalist, and a symbol of women's liberation. We're talking about a time when the act of a woman wearing pants was a revolutionary statement. Imagine that!

In 1840, Amelia Jenks married Dexter Bloomer. The marriage could be described as typical for the era—except for the unique dynamism of the two personalities involved. Dexter, an attorney, journalist, and editor of a local paper, advocated for temperance and other social reforms. Together, they relocated to Seneca Falls, a community that would become the birthplace of the American women's rights movement. Amelia, now Mrs Bloomer, was thrust into a world that allowed her to explore her capabilities beyond the confines of a schoolroom. But marriage isn't the ultimate validation for a woman. It may bring societal status, but it can also confine. For Amelia Bloomer, however, matrimony became a partnership that expanded her intellectual horizons.

Herein lies the crux: the marriage, far from diminishing Amelia, amplified her voice. Dexter recognized her talent and encouraged her to write for his paper, "The Seneca County Courier." Suddenly, her voice was not confined to the echoes of a classroom; it was in print, accessible to anyone who picked up a newspaper. Writing for the paper, Amelia started exploring social and moral concerns. It was as if each published article blew life into the embers of her social consciousness.

In 1849, something extraordinary happened. The Bloomers attended a talk by Elizabeth Cady Stanton, a women's rights movement figurehead. It was a cosmic intersection where two celestial bodies of activism aligned. Stanton's ideas not only resonated with Amelia but encouraged her. Amelia attended women's rights conventions and became deeply involved in the emerging movement. At this juncture, she launched her publication, "The Lily." Initially intended as a temperance journal, the magazine evolved to address various women's issues, from the right to vote to property rights. And yes, the magazine even talked about dress reform.

Let's not undervalue the role of "The Lily" in Amelia's life. It transformed her from a participant to a leader. She was no longer echoing the thoughts of others; she was creating a dialogue, leading conversations, and establishing herself as an authority. With a circulation reaching thousands, "The Lily" turned Amelia Bloomer into a household name.

So, what about those infamous bloomers? The costume that made her name synonymous with a controversial garment was not, in fact, her creation. But when Amelia started wearing the attire comprising a short skirt and full-cut trousers, she endorsed it through her platform in "The Lily." Wearing the bloomers was not merely a fashion statement but an expression of the belief that women should not be restricted—not in their clothing, roles, and certainly not in their ambitions.

Consider this: Amelia could've stopped at any point, stayed a teacher, and been content with a modest life in upstate New York. She could've settled for being Mrs. Dexter Bloomer. But she didn't. And this hunger, this relentless pursuit of more knowledge, freedom, and justice — propelled her to become a key player in a movement that would change the course of history.

Each article Amelia wrote, each convention she attended, and even each pair of bloomers she donned were not isolated actions. They were dots in a constellation, individual yet interconnected steps in the journey of a woman coming into her own. At times, public reactions to her ideas and dress were vehement, even scornful. But Amelia wasn't disheartened. Instead, she continued, aware that each article, each public appearance, each assertion of her right to live free of societal constraints was, in essence, an act of courage.

We can see that Amelia Bloomer's life was not one of ease. It was, however, a life lived with gusto, fueled by a deep-seated desire to make a difference. She wasn't just a woman of her time; she was ahead of her time, a woman who shaped her time. Reading Amelia's story means encountering a historical figure and meeting a woman whose courage and audacity resonate even today.

And so, as we contemplate this chapter of Amelia's life, we realize it wasn't merely an episode; it was an awakening, a 'Bloomer in Bloom,' if you will. A woman who seized her time and space and, in doing so, extended the boundaries for all women. Her story was not one of ease but one of relentless, fiery will. A will that burned so brightly couldn't help but set the world ablaze.

The Birth of the Bloomer Costume

Have you ever wondered how an ordinary garment could ascend to a symbol of revolution? In Amelia Bloomer's case, it wasn't the silk of the garment but the spirit woven into its threads that transformed a mere piece of clothing into a manifesto of female autonomy. In a society that constrained women's bodies in the suffocating layers of Victorian fashion, could a pair of trousers herald the beginnings of emancipation? The "Bloomer Costume" — a costume that played a role signified a stance — became an emblem of much more than sartorial choice; it became the cloth of contention, emblematic of a generation of women desperate for change.

Contrary to popular belief, Amelia Bloomer did not design the radical attire that came to be known as the "Bloomer costume." The honour of its invention belongs to Elizabeth Smith Miller, an American women's rights advocate. Miller, bothered by the impracticality and health risks of tight corsets and cumbersome skirts, sought a more sensible alternative. Enter the Bloomer costume, comprising a knee-length dress with baggy trousers peeping from underneath. An embodiment of functional fashion, if ever there was one.

But how did Amelia Bloomer enter this narrative? The meeting of Miller and Bloomer — set against the backdrop of the burgeoning women's rights movement — was nothing short of serendipitous. When Amelia first donned the outfit, she was immediately aware of the statement she was making. She was also aware of the backlash she might face. Still, Amelia was never one to shy away from controversy, was she?

It was Amelia's subsequent advocacy that catapulted this ensemble into the limelight. By featuring the garment in her newspaper, "The Lily," she lent it an air of legitimacy. She didn't just wear the Bloomer costume; she endorsed it, stood by it, and transformed it into a visual and ideological statement. That the costume came to be identified with her name rather than Miller's speaks volumes about Amelia's power to influence and galvanize. Amelia made the garment famous, but the garment also made Amelia a touchstone in a cultural debate.

Picture a woman in the 1850s, moving around freely, unburdened by layers of petticoats or the weight of societal norms. Amelia Bloomer might have walked with a slight hesitancy, keenly aware of the attention she drew. She might have felt the eyes, the scrutiny, the judgment, yet she wore her costume with pride. Her boldness lay in embracing a controversial fashion and understanding its broader implications. For Bloomer, the costume rejected the constricting norms forced upon women. It was more than just fabric; it was freedom, cut and stitched into form.

Let's address the elephant in the room: the public reaction. To say that it was mixed would be an understatement. The Bloomer costume became a flashpoint for heated societal debate. It was mocked in newspapers and criticized from pulpits. Yet, isn't that precisely where its power lay? In forcing society to articulate its discomforts to confront its prejudices, Amelia — and her Bloomer costume — was doing the heavy lifting for an entire movement. The criticism was fierce, but the conversation had started, which was a triumph.

But for all its significance, adopting the Bloomer costume was not universal, even within the ranks of the women's movement. Leaders like Susan B. Anthony and Elizabeth Cady Stanton initially adopted the attire. Still, they later reverted to traditional dress, fearing that the costume controversy overshadowed the broader goals of women's rights. Amelia herself eventually abandoned the dress, acknowledging its divisive impact, but only after ensuring that the conversation about women's autonomy had been irrevocably ignited.

Does the abandoning of the costume signify a defeat? Not in the least. Amelia knew when to pick her battles, when to push forward, and when to retreat. The Bloomer costume had served its purpose — as a provocative symbol, statement, and rallying point. The costume's disappearance from Amelia's wardrobe did not signify her ideas' retreat but their evolution.

Through this narrative lens, the birth of the Bloomer costume isn't just an intriguing fashion history anecdote; it's a chapter in the history of social progress. The garment might have eventually faded into sartorial history, but its ideological impact? That, my friends, is stitched into the fabric of women's rights, a legacy that persists.

Ah, Amelia. In the Bloomer costume, you gave us more than a garment; you gave us a gaze, a new way to see and be seen. You invited controversy, but you also invited change. And that's the lasting power of Amelia Bloomer — her ability to discern that in the minutiae, in something as everyday as what we wear, lie the seeds of revolution.

Fashion as Rebellion: The Symbolism of the Bloomer

Can a piece of cloth drape an ideology? When it comes to Amelia Bloomer and her eponymous "Bloomer costume," the answer is yes and resoundingly so. Adopting this garment wasn't just a fashion statement; it was an act of rebellion, a challenge to Victorian norms that went far beyond the sewing room to dissect and unsettle cultural mores.

What did women's fashion look like in the 1850s? Let's set the stage. Women were ensconced in crinolines and corsets, their bodies confined as neatly as their roles in society. The day's fashion was more than just clothing; it was a physical manifestation of societal constraints. Enter the Bloomer costume, a radical departure from these norms. Created by Elizabeth Smith Miller but popularized by Amelia, this outfit consisted of a loose-fitting tunic paired with voluminous trousers cinched at the ankle. A revolution in fabric.

Amelia encountered the outfit through her friend Elizabeth, and something clicked when she saw it. She didn't just see fabric; she saw possibility, an alignment of aesthetics and ethics. This wasn't just an alternative to oppressive fashion norms but a visual metaphor for all the changes she and her contemporaries were fighting for. Think about it: By replacing the skirts that weighed women down, weren't they also tossing aside the weight of gender expectations?

Amelia was an editor of "The Lily," a newspaper originally dedicated to temperance but gradually evolved into a broader platform for women's issues. Using this platform, Amelia became an evangelist for the Bloomer costume. She wrote about it; she published articles and illustrations portraying it. In her capable hands, the costume wasn't just endorsed; it was elevated to a form of sartorial civil disobedience. Just imagine: Every woman who donned the Bloomer wore her dissension, walking around in her rebellion. How many social norms did this simple act shatter?

The controversy generated by the Bloomer was electric. Newspaper articles lampooned it, and clerics denounced it from the pulpit. Social norms were not merely norms; they were fortresses, and here was Amelia Bloomer, lobbing her sartorial cannonballs. The garment took on layers of meaning it might never have had if it had merely stayed in the closet. By walking into the public square dressed in their convictions, women wearing the Bloomer were throwing down a challenge: Here we are, it said, different and unashamed.

But let's not gloss over the obstacles. Even within the women's rights movement, the Bloomer was divisive. Icons like Elizabeth Cady Stanton and Susan B. Anthony adopted it initially. Still, they reverted to conventional attire, anxious that this contentious garment was eclipsing the more significant causes of women's suffrage and legal rights. Amelia Bloomer stopped wearing it after a few years, concerned that the focus on fashion overshadowed the monumental societal issues. But consider this: Had the outfit not sparked such explosive debate, would we still be talking about it — and, by extension, the early women's rights movement — today?

Amelia understood the limitations of her iconic outfit. In laying it aside, she wasn't admitting defeat but shifting the battleground. The Bloomer had already done its work; it had ignited conversations, disrupted the status quo, and made the personal political. In its fabric were woven the threads of rebellion, individualism, and an insatiable desire for change.

So what do we make of the Bloomer's legacy? The trousers and tunic may have gone out of fashion, but the spirit they encapsulated survived. When we talk about fashion as a form of self-expression today, we're drawing on a discourse that women like Amelia Bloomer helped to initiate. It's not just what you wear but what you dare to represent that makes fashion a continual act of rebellion or conformity.

Amelia's Bloomers may no longer be the height of fashion or feminism. Still, their questions are as relevant now as they were then. They force us to ask ourselves: What are we willing to stand for, and what are we willing to put on to stand out? The Bloomer costume had its day in the sun. Yet, its rays are felt even now, in every piece of clothing that challenges the conventional wisdom, in every thread that aspires to be more than just a thread, but a statement. Amelia Bloomer gave us that, and it's a legacy that transcends any cut of cloth.

Public Reception and Controversy

Ah, the power of public opinion is an invisible but palpable force that can lift you to stardom or sink you into oblivion. What happens when a woman, a newspaper editor no less, decides to confront that force head-on, armed with nothing but a new style of clothing and a few columns in her publication? Let's peel back the layers, literally and metaphorically, to explore the turbulent public reception Amelia Bloomer faced when she donned and advocated for the audacious garment that would bear her name for posterity.

Was the Bloomer merely a fashion choice? Hardly. The moment Amelia started promoting this liberating costume through her newspaper, "The Lily," she stepped into a volatile arena. Not only did she challenge fashion, but she also dared to question the assumptions about femininity, etiquette, and freedom. Imagine stepping out of the house for a simple errand, only to be met with stares, pointing fingers, and hushed whispers. That's what Bloomer-wearing women faced. Each outing was transformed into a radical act, whether they liked it or not. And that's precisely what Amelia relished — the public couldn't ignore the issue.

So, how did the press react? Not kindly, for the most part. Editorial cartoons lampooned her, conservative newspaper columns criticized her, and religious leaders, ever the custodians of morality, sermonized against her audacious threads. The criticisms were against a new fashion trend but against an imagined collapse of social mores. The clothing was viewed as symptomatic of a moral failing, a rebellion against dresses and traditional womanhood. How could trousers lead to such turmoil, you ask? In the rigid context of 19th-century America, clothing was more than fabric; it was a language, a set of signs and symbols loaded with meaning.

But, mind you, it wasn't all brickbats. Amelia's pioneering endeavour garnered support from unlikely quarters. Other suffragists initially adopted the Bloomer; even a few brave men penned columns in its favour. However, what remains intriguing is that despite the backlash and the ridicule, the debate surrounding the Bloomer never waned during its years of prominence. Amelia had captured the national imagination, hadn't she? And if her trousers were the source of humour and disdain, they were also a subject of curiosity, discussion, and even, albeit reluctantly, admiration. The Bloomer was controversial because it was compelling; it engaged the public in a conversation many didn't even realize needed to be had.

You'd think Amelia would remain unbowed amid this tumult, wouldn't you? Yet even this indomitable spirit found herself weighing the costs. After a time, Amelia did distance herself from the garment that had captivated and horrified a nation. But don't mistake this shift for a retreat; it was a recalibration. Amelia realized the garment had eclipsed broader, more pressing issues of women's rights. In her wisdom, Amelia saw that the battle for equality wouldn't be won or lost on trousers alone. She continued to edit "The Lily," still advocating for women's suffrage and temperance but with a slightly subdued focus on the controversial garb. This doesn't mean she gave in but chose her battles wisely.

The rollercoaster of public reception that Amelia experienced showcased the weight of cultural symbols.

Clothing can be laden with assumptions and expectations far beyond personal preference. Amelia had rocked the boat but navigated the choppy waters of public opinion with an oar of resilience and a compass of conviction. Whether you see her as a martyr to her cause or as a savvy operator who understood the tides of public opinion, the fact remains: Amelia Bloomer thrust the debate about women's rights into public consciousness using the most unlikely weapon — a pair of billowy pants. She may have retreated from the battlefield of fashion. Still, in doing so, she gained a stronger footing in the war for women's equality.

So, what's the takeaway? Amelia Bloomer's experience with public reception was an object lesson in the potent mix of clothing, gender, and societal norms. Her story is not just about a short-lived fashion trend; it's a vivid narrative of resistance and adaptation. And though the Bloomer costume may have faded away, the discourse it sparked — the fierce debates, the challenging of norms, the audacity of change — continues to resonate. Amelia didn't just change her clothes; she changed the conversation. Isn't that the hallmark of a true icon?

Intellectual Exchanges and Influences

The path to intellectual ferment often winds through interactions and exchanges of ideas that challenge the mind to expand its boundaries. Now, imagine being a woman in the early 19th century. A staid society expects you to occupy the domestic sphere. Still, you yearn for more — a voice, an influence, a stake in your country's social and political fabric. How do you find your tribe in such an environment? That's the difficulty Amelia Bloomer faced, and her solution came through intellectual exchanges that both influenced her and allowed her to exert her influence.

Seneca Falls, New York, was not just any American town; it was a hotbed of social reform and intellectual discourse, especially in the 1840s and 1850s. This milieu would play a significant role in shaping Amelia's convictions. Moving there after her marriage, Amelia soon found herself in a circle that included Elizabeth Cady Stanton and Lucretia Mott, women whose names would be etched into history for their audacious challenges to the status quo. A web of letters, articles, and face-to-face debates flowed among these women and their broader circle. Each discussion was a brick in the edifice of Amelia's burgeoning social and intellectual life.

But don't picture Amelia as a mere acolyte, passively absorbing the influences around her. She actively participated in these dialogues, contributing her original ideas. When she took over the helm of "The Lily," a periodical focused on temperance, she began steering its content toward broader issues of women's rights and suffrage. The paper became a platform for dialogue, bringing the conversation about women's roles out of private parlours and into a more public, shareable domain. Isn't it fascinating how a small publication could have such an outsized impact on public opinion?

One cannot neglect the import of Amelia's husband, Dexter Bloomer — a supportive man in an era when such support was hard to come by. While not an intellectual influence in the traditional sense, his influence was palpable in the space he gave Amelia to grow intellectually. How many women of that era were denied the resources and freedom to cultivate their minds simply because their spouses held tight to society's reins? Dexter Bloomer was different. He admired Amelia's intellect, provided her with books and resources, and, most importantly, respected her autonomy.

What, then, about Amelia Bloomer's intellectual legacy? How did her ideas continue to resonate? Her endorsement of what became known as the "Bloomer costume" is a testament to her ability to combine sartorial and intellectual innovation, compelling society to confront its norms. While Amelia eventually distanced herself from the Bloomer, the garment had already done its job. It forced society to take women seriously as agents capable of making trivial and significant choices. And let's not forget, she did this while navigating a labyrinth of social mores designed to stifle such freedom.

Moreover, Amelia's stint as an editor helped amplify voices that might otherwise have been marginalized. Susan B. Anthony, another towering figure in the suffrage movement, credited Amelia's influence, mainly how "The Lily" created a space for a discourse on women's suffrage. It would be Susan B. Anthony and Elizabeth Cady Stanton who would carry the torch forward. Still, the flame was, in part, lit by Amelia.

Intellectual exchanges are not just debates or arguments; they are the oxygen that fuels the fire of social change. Amelia Bloomer understood this viscerally. She not only breathed in the radical ideas of her era but also breathed out her own, thus creating a cyclical wind of change that fanned the flames of reform. This milieu of give-and-take, this fertile ground of intellectual fervour, enabled Amelia to grow from a curious young woman into an emblem of resistance and reform.

She didn't just live in her era; she helped define it. She didn't merely absorb influences; she became an influence. And though the fabric of her famous garment has long since frayed, the threads of her intellectual legacy are woven into the very tapestry of American thought. A tapestry that Amelia Bloomer would likely look upon with pride. After all, isn't that what intellectual exchange is all about — leaving an indelible imprint long after you've moved on?

The Seneca Falls Convention: A Crucible of Convictions

How often does a seemingly ordinary meeting in an otherwise forgettable town ignite a revolution? When it comes to the Seneca Falls Convention, held in July 1848, the answer is a resounding "once is enough." For Amelia Bloomer, a woman poised on the edge of a metamorphosis, this event was not just another page in the calendar but a pivotal moment in her life.

In a two-story building called the Wesleyan Chapel, people gathered, some out of curiosity, others with a purpose. Little did they know that they were stepping into history. Amelia Bloomer, too, stepped through those doors, her breath likely held in a mix of anticipation and anxiety. Here was a woman who had already shown her commitment to social causes like temperance, but this was something else. Women's rights, suffrage, property rights — these were topics that society had swept under the rug for far too long.

Now, picture this: Elizabeth Cady Stanton stands before the crowd, articulating her thoughts with an eloquence born of long-suppressed fury. What went through Amelia's mind as she listened? Can we even begin to understand the alchemy of emotions — hope, fear, exhilaration — that were undoubtedly fusing inside her? Stanton read out the Declaration of Sentiments, a daring adaptation of the Declaration of Independence, only this time, "mankind" was replaced with "womankind." Each grievance aired, and each resolution declared probably struck Amelia like a lightning bolt of revelation.

While many convention attendees hesitated to sign the document — some out of disbelief, others due to societal pressures — Amelia was not among them, far from it. She was entering a crucible of activism and transformation, and the fire was lit. She later recalled that moment as a crystallizing event, saying, "I realized as never before the wrongs women have suffered." With each signature, the Declaration gained more power. Amelia's signature was an indelible mark of her growing commitment to women's liberation.

Here's what's truly remarkable. In the following years, Amelia didn't just ride the wave initiated at Seneca Falls; she became one of its most formidable forces. Many convention attendees returned to their routines, but Amelia had changed irrevocably. Her experiences and encounters during that gathering acted like kindling to the fire of her activism. Seneca Falls wasn't just a place or an event for Amelia; it was a catalyst. What was once a flicker of dissatisfaction with society's norms had now ignited a flame of defiance.

The questions raised and answered at Seneca Falls were pillars of Amelia's crusade for women's rights. Her periodical, "The Lily," for instance, expanded its focus from temperance to include these broader issues. Did Amelia start "The Lily" because of Seneca Falls? No. But after this convention, her journalistic endeavours gained fervour and an unmistakable focus on women's suffrage and rights. It was like a clarion call had sounded. Amelia, who had already contemplated these issues in her work, now had the affirmation she needed to expand her reach and deepen her voice.

Ah, the power of moments — how they can change the course of a single life and impact countless others. As Seneca Falls acted as a cornerstone of the women's rights movement, it served as a personal watershed for Amelia. Post-convention, she didn't just advocate; she became a symbol. Her advocacy bore the hallmark of someone whose convictions had been intensely fortified by a transformative experience.

Indeed, life is a series of events, some monumental, others mundane. But there are rare occasions when the monumental and the mundane converge to create something extraordinary. For Amelia Bloomer, the Seneca Falls Convention was one such extraordinary event. It didn't merely inform her activism; it galvanized it. She went in as a woman mindful of the inequities of her time and came out as a crusader with her resolve set in stone. And in doing so, Amelia didn't just attend a convention; she participated in a revolution. Isn't that the ultimate triumph — to witness history and help shape it?

Chapter 4

A Pen Mightier than Petticoats

The dawn of 1849 must have found Amelia Bloomer in a reflective mood.

Only a few months since she'd participated in the groundbreaking Seneca Falls Convention, the winds of change had set her course in an entirely new direction. The question that confronted her was not whether she should act but how. How could she lend her voice to this sprawling tapestry of reform? And in what way could she, a woman in the male-dominated society of the 19th century, make a substantive impact?

The Lily: A Platform for Change

Can you imagine a world where the pen becomes an extension of one's soul, where ink spills not just words but revolutions? Amelia Bloomer lived in such a universe, scribing her reality into existence through a newspaper that served as a nucleus of change. "The Lily," it was called — a name delicate in its simplicity yet resilient in its purpose.

Picture Amelia in her study, a room that's likely small and unassuming but filled with the scents of ink and the tangible aspirations of a woman determined to make a difference. How many evenings must she have spent there, penning articles in the dim light, each stroke an act of defiance against the oppressive norms of her era? She wasn't just composing articles but laying bricks for the foundation of women's rights.

Enter "The Lily," a newspaper Amelia had begun the year before, initially to discuss temperance — a safe topic. But here, in this stack of paper and ink, lay an uncharted world. Could a publication be the channel she had been seeking? Amelia must have sensed the untapped potential of the capacity of written words to shape ideas and drive action. Words, after all, could travel places she couldn't; they could infiltrate drawing rooms and cafes, forcing people to confront the uncomfortable questions they would rather avoid.

"The Lily" was about to undergo a seismic shift. Amelia had caught the spirit of Seneca Falls, that incendiary fusion of ideas and action, and channelled it into her writing. Come spring of 1849, you could feel a change in the air. It wasn't just the buds on the trees or the thawing ground but the words Amelia Bloomer printed in "The Lily." Suddenly, the pages were buzzing with talks about women's right to vote, laws that kept women in chains, and the societal expectations that made wives seem like mere accessories to their husbands. It was as if Amelia had thrown open the windows of a stuffy room, letting in a fresh breeze that shook the curtains and made you sit up a little straighter in your chair.

The newspaper wasn't just sheets of inked paper anymore; it had transformed into Amelia's stage. Alongside her like-minded peers, she used those pages to perform a performance that dared to question their very world. A publication that had begun under the auspices of temperance had suddenly started to roar with feminist undertones.

But why the focus on women's issues in a temperance paper? The connection was more organic than it might seem initially. Women were often the most afflicted by the consequences of excessive drinking. Yet, they had no legal standing to divorce a husband or claim property. In highlighting this disparity, Amelia displayed a masterful sleight of hand: She linked the temperance cause to the more significant issue of women's rights, effortlessly melding two significant movements of her time.

Not everyone was thrilled, of course. Detractors were quick to label her an extremist, a rabble-rouser. Amelia had hit a nerve, and the backlash began to pour in. "The Lily," once a placid temperance gazette, was now controversial. But isn't that the point of activism, after all? To disrupt, challenge, and make people uncomfortable until change becomes preferable and inevitable?

Yet Amelia's influence didn't stop at the newspaper. By 1851, she had become associated with a style of dress that defied convention. Women's attire in the 19th century was cumbersome — layers of petticoats, restrictive corsets, and long skirts that scraped the floor. When Amelia saw the more practical clothing her friend Elizabeth Smith Miller promoted, she immediately recognized its utility. What followed was one of the earliest instances of celebrity endorsement. Amelia started wearing the garments, wrote about them in "The Lily," and even her name became synonymous with the style — "Bloomers."

It's easy to dismiss this as a fashion statement but consider what Amelia was doing momentarily. She was challenging deeply ingrained norms, just as she did in her writings. The uproar over the new dress style was about more than aesthetics or comfort; it was about the freedom to exist in the world without literally and metaphorically burdened by layers of restrictive fabric. Amelia wasn't just comfortable in trousers and a short skirt; she was radical.

The new attire led to another wave of public scrutiny. Cartoons were published, mocking her; debates raged in the press. Amelia remained unfazed. Like her editorial choices in "The Lily," her clothing was a statement of freedom, an extension of her ideology. In a way, Amelia Bloomer had discovered the symbiosis between form and function, between a woman's right to comfort and her right to voice her opinion.

As the years rolled on, Amelia continued to push boundaries. She never severed her ties with temperance but allowed her activism to grow more complex and nuanced, creating a composite picture of the challenges women faced. Through her newspaper, she lent her support to the suffragettes, and her name remained linked to the transformative power of ideas. By penning provocative and informed articles, Amelia effectively turned "The Lily" into a spearhead of the women's movement.

Ultimately, Amelia's legacy was twofold: a pen unafraid to challenge and attire that refused to conform. The two might seem disparate, but they were inextricably connected on the canvas of 19th-century America. Amelia Bloomer demonstrated through her words and deeds that the mightiest weapon against injustice is the courage to stand against the tide. And in doing so, she not only chronicled history; she helped shape it. Isn't that what we all hope to achieve in our limited time on this earth — to leave an imprint that says we were here, we mattered, and we made a difference?

Let's step back a bit. "The Lily" didn't start as a feminist juggernaut. Amelia Bloomer launched it in 1849, ostensibly to discuss temperance — a crucial issue of the day, especially for women who bore the brunt of alcohol-induced domestic violence. However, like a river that begins as a meagre stream but ultimately turns into a torrent, the content of "The Lily" evolved. It swelled with Amelia's burgeoning realization that the personal was political. And so, from the narrow scope of temperance, "The Lily" blossomed into a platform that tackled women's rights, suffrage, and social norms, among other issues.

Why this transition, you ask? Well, think of the period Amelia lived in. She was embedded in a society that treated women as second-class citizens, denied them the right to vote, and constricted them into roles as mere wives and mothers. Amelia knew that the issues were interconnected — alcoholism wasn't just a disease; it was a symptom of a deeper social malaise that wouldn't be cured unless women had a say in their destinies. Was it so surprising that her newspaper would transcend its original agenda?

Importantly, Amelia wasn't alone. She was part of an intricate web of intellectuals and activists — Elizabeth Cady Stanton, Susan B. Anthony, and many others. Her newspaper began featuring contributions from these luminaries, becoming a hallowed ground of shared visions and aspirations. Isn't it fascinating how ideas can feed off each other, gaining momentum until they become unstoppable?

Now, publishing a newspaper is one thing; getting people to read it is another. How did Amelia accomplish this feat? She did it through a mix of audacity and wit, employing an editorial style that was assertive yet approachable. She would pose questions, challenge the reader's preconceptions, and often employ anecdotes and examples that made complex issues relatable. Her writing was imbued with urgency — you could almost hear her saying, "We must act, and we must act now."

Was everyone pleased with Amelia's audacious move to change the thematic focus of her newspaper? Of course not. Amelia knew the art of shaking the tree and was prepared for the falling apples. Critics began labelling her an extremist, an instigator of social discord. But she didn't flinch. For every critic, countless women felt seen, heard, and empowered by "The Lily." Indeed, these women became the backbone of an emergent movement galvanized by a humble newspaper that had dared to speak truth to power.

In many ways, "The Lily" served as a mirror of Amelia's metamorphosis. The woman who had moved to Seneca Falls as a young bride, uncertain about her place in a world driven by men, was now leading a revolution through words. Yes, her advocacy spanned beyond the newspaper — from her famous adoption of the "Bloomer" attire to her active participation in suffrage movements — but "The Lily" remained her most consistent tool for change. It was her pulpit, stage, and open letter to the world.

And let's not underestimate the courage it took to sustain such a publication. Every new issue of "The Lily" was an act of rebellion, a jab at the status quo. By embracing topics considered 'unladylike,' Amelia Bloomer did more than publish a newspaper; she defied an entire social structure. Could there be anything more revolutionary?

The years rolled on, but Amelia's determination remained steadfast. Eventually, she had to relinquish the editorial reins of "The Lily" due to her relocation to Ohio. But by then, her newspaper had already laid down a memorable framework for feminist journalism. Even after Amelia, "The Lily" continued to serve as a platform for women's voices, a historical record of a time when women were forging their destiny.

And so, "The Lily" remains an enduring testament to Amelia Bloomer's vision. Every line penned in that newspaper was a stepping stone on the path to equality, each issue a ripple in the pond of social consciousness. Amelia Bloomer showed us the might of a humble newspaper in challenging the citadels of patriarchy. Through "The Lily," she didn't just make history; she shaped it. In the end, wasn't that the most profound statement she could make?

Advocacy through Journalism

What does it take to lend a voice to the voiceless? To spark a revolution with mere words, to draw lines not just on a page but in the sand? Amelia Bloomer had a clue. A journalist by vocation but a crusader at heart, she found her medium in newsprint and her message in ink. This isn't just a story of a woman who wrote; this is about a woman who wrote things into being.

When Amelia Bloomer launched "The Lily" in 1849, it was a sea change, yet hardly anyone realized it. Initially dedicated to the temperance movement, this publication was not the first of its kind, but the woman behind it was. She saw what others could not: a newspaper, even a modest one, could be a galvanizing force for social change. After all, what is a newspaper but a dialogue with society? This running conversation has the power to change minds and reshape public opinion? But how did she transition from a woman who hesitated to speak in public gatherings to one who orchestrated debates through journalism?

Amelia's involvement in temperance was the catalyst, but her vision was broader. Rooted in her was a nascent but growing understanding that societal ailments were not just about men drowning in alcohol but also about women drowning in inequality. Temperance was only one symptom of a disease called "injustice." And Amelia decided to diagnose this ailment in the most public way she could: through journalism.

Imagine the time and context. The 19th-century United States was a cauldron of social and political ferment. Slavery, women's suffrage, labour rights — these were not just issues; they were wars fought in households and public squares alike. Amelia Bloomer positioned "The Lily" as a stronghold amid this chaos. The newspaper became her platform for discussing temperance and matters like women's rights, suffrage, and marriage laws. Think of the audacity it took to do this — to transform a single-issue paper into a diverse platform that encapsulated an emerging feminist consciousness.

Amelia's journalism was unique because it combined clarity with compassion. The words were her own, but the issues were everyone's. Whether advocating for women's right to vote or discussing the restrictive nature of women's clothing (yes, the famous 'Bloomers' take their name from her), her prose didn't just inform; it incited action. She spoke not just to the intellect but to the soul. Each article, each editorial was an invitation: "Come, be a part of this change."

Critics came, as they always do when the status quo is challenged. People called her a radical as if she were launching a full-scale attack on the time-honoured traditions everyone held dear. Every word she penned in journalism was seen as a direct challenge to how things were "supposed" to be. What does it say about us when a woman's wish for equal footing with men gets labelled "radical"? Imagine that. In a room full of ideas, the one that dares to suggest women are equal citizens — that's the one that sends eyebrows arching toward the ceiling. Makes you wonder, doesn't it? What are we terrified of when a woman asks for nothing more than to stand on the same ground as a man? Amelia Bloomer, however, had a spine of steel. Criticism didn't deter her; it fueled her. Her editorial choices became bolder, her voice louder, and her pen sharper.

It wasn't a monologue, however. "The Lily" became a fertile ground for other voices advocating change. Contributions from other leading women of the time, like Elizabeth Cady Stanton and Susan B. Anthony, graced its pages. Amelia Bloomer recognized the power of collective action, the might that comes from unity. She was savvy enough to realize that "The Lily" could serve as a rallying point, a sanctuary of thought for like-minded women. In doing this, she turned the paper into something far more significant than herself—a wave of change that would continue long after she was gone.

The impact of her work in journalism ripples out way past the boundaries of her 19th-century world, like a stone tossed into a still pond, creating waves that reach us even today. As a pioneering woman journalist and publisher, Amelia laid the groundwork for the journalists who followed, both male and female. While she might have been one of the first women to own, operate, and edit a newspaper for women, the tradition did not end with her. Think about that — the memorable, rippling effect of one woman's audacity.

Now, the pages of "The Lily" have yellowed with time, the ink has faded, and the typefaces are styles of a bygone era. But the words? Ah, the words still resonate, as fresh as the day they were printed. Amelia Bloomer showed us the transformative power of journalism: A newspaper could be more than just paper — it could be a manifesto, a movement, or a life. And for women confined to the margins of history, she offered the most potent weapon: a voice. How could anyone ever silence us after that?

The Power of the Printed Word

How do you break barriers? How do you tell a society, entrenched in its ways, that change isn't just good — it's essential? You give them the printed word, handed to them by Amelia Bloomer. If journalism is the first rough draft of history,

Amelia was at her writing desk, rolling ink onto the parchment of societal norms.

It's crucial to appreciate the world Amelia Bloomer found herself in. It was a world of hushed parlours and shuttered windows for women, where 'respectability' dictated almost every aspect of their lives. But Amelia wasn't content to be a whisper; she wanted to be a shout. And she chose the printed word as her megaphone.

Why did Bloomer turn to the printing press? Could she have chosen a more modest, less aggressive approach? Perhaps. But the newspaper was the internet of her era. This viral medium could reach the parlours and the pubs, the young and the old, with equal efficacy. It was a platform with undeniable reach and unparalleled influence. So, imagine Amelia rolling up her sleeves, ready to dive into the issues that mattered. She would use her newspaper like a megaphone, blasting out calls for women's rights, making a case for temperance, and rallying folks toward social justice. She wasn't just planning to nudge society; she aimed to shake it by its roots.

Amelia Bloomer started her journalistic journey with "The Lily," a publication modest in size but not ambition. Her newspaper offered something utterly different from the florid prose and mundane domesticity found in most women's magazines of the time. Each issue was a rhetorical cannonball shot across the bow of 19th-century American patriarchy. Even though it began as a temperance journal, Bloomer saw her platform as far more. "The Lily" would soon blossom into a vocal advocate for women's suffrage, educational rights, and —

to much public consternation — a rethinking of women's fashion.

Amelia Bloomer understood the potent alchemy of ink and paper and the printed word's transformational power. Every column she wrote, every issue she published, wasn't just a collection of articles but a challenge — to her readers, society, and herself. She dissected the issues of her time with a razor-sharp pen, offering compelling arguments and incisive commentary that went far beyond mere reportage. And when you leaf through those ancient, yellowed pages today, the ink may have faded, but the power of the ideas has not. They still stir something in us.

Consider this: Bloomer didn't just pen articles. She was a curator of contemporary thought, inviting contributions from other social reformers of her era, like Elizabeth Cady Stanton and Susan B. Anthony. In doing so, she amplified the power of the printed word by making "The Lily" a kaleidoscope of voices, each adding a different hue to the spectrum of social advocacy. How many movements were sparked over a morning coffee and a read-through of "The Lily"? How many minds were opened, and how many conversations were started?

"The Lily" was a commercial endeavour, but the currency it traded in wasn't just money; it was changed. Amelia Bloomer commercialized the revolution, mainstreaming it into American homes in a digestible format that could be debated and discussed. Her paper was, after all, a business. And yet, the bottom line for her was always measured in societal change, not merely in subscriptions and ad revenue.

Controversy and criticism were constant companions for Bloomer. The traditionalists and the conservatives saw her not as an agent of change but as a harbinger of chaos. And it's easy to vilify what you don't understand. Amelia Bloomer, however, never saw controversy as a barrier; she saw it as an indicator that she was effectively hitting a nerve, challenging the status quo. Criticism didn't blunt her pen; it sharpened it. Each critique was a call to reevaluate, to reformulate, but never to retreat.

Would Amelia have had the impact she did without the medium of the printed word? It's tempting to think of alternate histories where she might have chosen another path — perhaps oratory or direct activism. But it was the immediacy and accessibility of the printed word that set her apart. This choice allowed her to reach into the homes and hearts of Americans, both the sympathetic and the sceptical. To make them confront uncomfortable questions every time they unfolded a new edition of "The Lily." To plant seeds of change in the fertile ground of public consciousness.

Amelia Bloomer demonstrated that the pen could be mightier than the sword and often more cutting than spoken words. She showed that ideas, once committed to print, were impossible to erase. It was in the newspaper columns, in the clatter of the printing press and in the sharp smell of fresh ink that Amelia found her true power.

Through journalism, Amelia Bloomer did more than inform; she transformed. She made people question, wonder, and sometimes angrily debate. But most importantly, she made them think. And in the stillness that follows the turning of a page, in that pause, before we move on to the following article or task, it's there that Amelia Bloomer's legacy truly lies — in the conversations she started that we still have today.

Chapter 5

The Dance of Matrimony

What does it say about a woman who steps out of the tulle and silk of her own wedding gown and into the ink and parchment of activism? Picture Amelia Bloomer, young and brimming with ideas, saying "I do", not just to her husband but also to a cause that could consume her very being. Now, is that not the quintessential marriage of passion and purpose?

Amelia Bloomer was not merely a wife in the traditional 19th-century sense. Marriage for her wasn't just an institution but more like a partnership. She married Dexter Bloomer, a man involved in the newspaper business, which presented a pivotal shift in her life. What might have been a happy conclusion to a Jane Austen novel was, for Amelia, a beginning of another chapter — one she'd write herself. Dexter didn't just share his life with Amelia; he shared his world of words, typefaces, and the incessant chatter of printing presses.

The move to Seneca Falls shortly after their wedding in 1840 served as the backdrop to Amelia's newfound ambitions. Ah, Seneca Falls! The place where a ripple in a pond would soon grow into a tidal wave of social reform. How could Amelia, a new bride, resist the pull of the social currents swirling around her? She couldn't. The zeitgeist of the era ran through her veins, urging her to be more than just Mrs. Dexter Bloomer.

One might assume that Dexter would be the overshadowing figure, the man whose career would drown out his partner's voice. But no, Dexter was not that kind of man. He saw the brilliance in Amelia — the fire in her eyes when she spoke about women's rights, the careful deliberation with which she considered social justice issues. How many husbands of that era would do the same? Dexter not only recognized Amelia's gifts but encouraged them.

It was in the welcoming arms of matrimony that Amelia found her platform. Her husband's involvement in the 'Seneca Falls Courier' offered her an inroad to journalism. Initially, she considered using her husband's platform to echo her thoughts. But why be the echo when you can be the voice? So was born "The Lily," Amelia's own newspaper and a milestone in the feminist movement. "Here, within these pages," she must have thought, "I'll build my arena."

"The Lily" wasn't merely a publication; it was a pulsating heart that pumped ideas into the veins of a society thirsty for change. Amelia used it to talk about subjects close to her, such as temperance and, most importantly, women's suffrage. Remember, this is an era where women were thought to belong in the kitchen and nursery, not in the newsroom. And yet, there she was, fighting against all odds.

The written word is like a dancer, isn't it? It moves across a page as feet do on a stage, each step intentional, each twirl calculated to provoke thought. With the dance of matrimony, Amelia had joined a partner who could match her stride for stride in the intricate choreography of life. Together, they produced a dance that pleased the eye and stirred the soul.

Can you sense the synergy there? A husband and wife duo, walking hand-in-hand, yet with enough space between their fingers for individual dreams to grow. What's a family, if not a collection of diverse dreams under a single roof?

The dance of matrimony is often viewed as a series of concessions, of give-and-take. But for Amelia, it was a collaborative ballet, where she and her partner both took turns leading and following. And let us not overlook that Amelia composed her own music in a society that often demanded women to dance to the tunes set by men.

So, in the grand tapestry of Amelia Bloomer's life, her marriage wasn't a mere ornamental knot; it was a crucial stitch that held together multiple layers of her existence. The woman who once stood at the altar in matrimonial bliss would soon stand on platforms, advocating for her sisters' rights. And behind her, always, was the man she chose to marry — a man who never asked her to be anything less than she was, who, indeed, encouraged her to be everything she could be.

The dance of matrimony? For Amelia Bloomer, it was less a dance and more an orchestrated revolution. A revolution that began at an altar and reverberated through the pages of 'The Lily,' across the stages of suffragette conventions, and into the lives of countless women. Amelia and Dexter Bloomer's matrimony was a partnership in the truest sense — a harmonious alignment of values, aspirations, and, most importantly, love. What more could one ask from a marriage, especially in a time that often asked women to ask for less?

Now, how's that for a love story? It is a story not of a woman lost in love but of a woman found — in love, in purpose, and in the ink that would write the future.

Dudley Bloomer: An Unconventional Match

What does it mean to find one's match? For Amelia Bloomer, it wasn't the type of courtship sprinkled with idyllic strolls and sentimental poetry you'd expect from a 19th-century romance. No, her match was Dudley Bloomer, a man as unconventional in his thinking as she was.

Now, imagine the scene — Amelia, a woman already in her late twenties, not exactly a desirable age for marriage, meeting Dudley, a man associated with the newspaper business. Ah, newspapers! The fascinating world where ideas take shape and dialogues spark change. Was it love at first sight? Maybe not, but it was a meeting of minds waiting to intersect.

Dudley wasn't your run-of-the-mill 19th-century man. Many men of that era believed in assigning roles, reducing women to mere extensions of themselves. Dudley? He chose to differ. He viewed Amelia not as someone who would cook his meals and bear his children but as an intellectual equal, a partner who could challenge him in conversations as comfortably as she could share his life.

But Dudley's unconventionality wasn't just confined to his personal attitudes. Professionally, he could have been more atypical. As editor of the "Seneca Falls Courier," Dudley had already made his mark in journalism. So, it was inevitable that Amelia, a woman brimming with ideas and opinions, would find a natural outlet in this field. They were like two pieces of a jigsaw puzzle — different in form, yet fitting perfectly together. Isn't that what a good match should be?

When Amelia stepped into matrimony, she also stepped into a world that opened endless possibilities. Here's where the couple's collective genius came alive. A newspaper man marries a woman with a mind bursting with unarticulated opinions, and what do you get? "The Lily" — a publication where Amelia could finally let her thoughts blossom. Would "The Lily" have been possible without Dudley? It's a question worth asking. While Amelia was the writer, the advocate, and the dreamer, Dudley was the enabler. This man provided the tools but never dictated how they should be used.

So, what did Dudley see in Amelia? For him, Amelia was not a woman to be shielded from the world; she was the one to present it with new paradigms. He saw in her a fellow traveller on the rugged terrain of social reform. Love, for them, was not a confining room but a sprawling landscape where each could explore their individual horizons even as they walked hand-in-hand.

One must consider the times to truly appreciate Dudley's exceptionalism. He encouraged Amelia to carve out her identity in an era that saw women as dependent beings. In a society that preached temperance for women, he stood by as Amelia advocated for it through her writings. Dudley, you see, was not merely a spectator in Amelia's life; he was an active participant. The world saw them as husband and wife, but they were co-conspirators in a lifelong mission to effect change.

Have you ever considered what a relationship could be if it broke free from society's preconceived moulds? If it did, it would look like Amelia and Dudley's union. A marriage that was not just a joining of two souls but a merging of visions.

And so, Dudley became Amelia's life partner in the truest sense. His newspaper, initially, was the canvas upon which Amelia began to sketch her ideas. Still, later, she would move on to her own ventures. Dudley's love did not try to bind Amelia; instead, it freed her. He was her confidant, advisor, harshest critic, and most ardent supporter — all rolled into one
.

Their marriage wasn't just an event that occurred one fine day in front of a clergyman. It was a dynamic, evolving pact. One thing remained constant through the ups and downs of their shared life: their dedication to each other and the causes they held dear. For Amelia, marriage was not an obstacle to her ambitions but rather the vehicle that propelled her into the public sphere. And much of that was possible because of the man she had by her side, Dudley, her unconventional match.

Can we pause momentarily and wonder what would have happened if Amelia had married a man of conventional beliefs? Would she have ever found the courage to enter the limelight, pen her convictions, and fight for what she believed in? Likely not. Dudley was more than Amelia's husband; he was her partner in a shared journey of discovery and advocacy.

In this tale of Amelia Bloomer, Dudley shines not as a mere footnote but as a compelling chapter of his own. This chapter underlines the power of companionship, the beauty of an unconventional match, and the endless possibilities that open up when two like-minded people decide to share a life. So, when we speak of Amelia Bloomer, let's not forget the man who stood beside her, who never tried to overshadow her but instead offered her a spotlight all her own.

And that's Dudley for you — not just a husband, but a visionary in his own right, one who saw the sparkle in Amelia long before the world would come to recognize it. A sparkle that, combined with his own, ignited a bright flame that would light the way for generations to come.

Love, Marriage, and the Bloomer Home

Have you ever thought about the alchemy of love and activism? Amelia Bloomer, born in 1818, didn't merely ponder this; she lived it. Imagine the times she inhabited — a period that so rigidly defined what a woman should be, what she could do, and what she could even wear. Yet here was Amelia, going against the grain, married to Dudley Bloomer, a partner as extraordinary as she was. But what kind of heart does an unconventional couple like Amelia and Dudley create?

Their marriage was less a domestic arrangement and more a pact of mutual respect and shared ideals. In Seneca Falls, New York, their home wasn't just a residence but a nucleus of social and intellectual gathering, the ground zero of many transformative ideas. How many dinners must have started with casual conversation and ended with debates that would echo in the history books?

The Bloomer household was no 19th-century tableau of domestic servitude. Amelia was not one to be relegated to the kitchen and nursery. Her home was her stage, where she scripted her thoughts, shared her ideals, and planned her actions. Dudley, an editor by trade, respected Amelia's individuality so much that he empowered her to launch her own paper, "The Lily."

Think about that. In an era where women were often confined to sewing circles, Amelia ran an editorial roundtable in her home. With Dudley's support, she transformed their domestic space into a workshop of ideas and activism. Can we just pause to imagine the evenings at the Bloomer home? Dudley editing his own newspaper and Amelia scribbling down her thoughts for "The Lily" — both fuelled by the passion to ignite change, both challenging and enriching each other's perspectives.

And let's not gloss over the significance of the space Amelia carved out within her home. She penned many of her revolutionary ideas about women's rights and temperance here. This home was where Amelia would don her infamous "bloomers," the loose-fitting, pants-like garments that became an audacious statement of female emancipation. The couple may have used ink for writing, but their ideas on equality and freedom were etched into the very walls of their home.

Amelia and Dudley nurtured a relationship that transcended the norms of their time. It was a partnership founded on intellectual camaraderie and a mutual longing for societal change. Isn't that what love should be at its core? A force that enriches both parties and, in the process, brings something new into the world?

Their love story remains an inspiring testament to the possibilities that open up when two people view each other as equals. But it wasn't just about them. Their home often welcomed other thinkers and activists — Elizabeth Cady Stanton and Susan B. Anthony — whose voices would become instrumental in the fight for women's rights. In this sense, the Bloomer home was not just a sanctuary for Amelia and Dudley but for the principles of freedom, equality, and intellectual pursuit.

And the children? Their son was raised in an atmosphere of vibrant discussion and progressive ideals. For young minds, the environment in which you grow up shapes your view of the world. Can you imagine being raised in such a stimulating setting? The son of Amelia and Dudley was growing up in a home where he not only heard but saw the principles of equality and activism practised daily. If homes are the foundational schools of society, then their home was a university of progressive thought.

But what does all of this tell us about the relationship between Amelia and Dudley? At the risk of veering into the speculative, one could argue that their shared vision fortified their love. The home they built was a testament to the symbiotic relationship they had, one where love, intellect, and activism were tightly interwoven.

In a time when many women had to choose between marriage and freedom, Amelia found both in her home with Dudley. Their domestic life was not a sanctuary away from the world but a command centre from which they launched into it. It's hard to think of a more radical statement than that, isn't it?

Two people united not just in matrimony but in a shared mission to reshape the world — all from the four walls of their home.

Indeed, Dudley was not merely Amelia's husband but an ally in her lifelong crusade. This wasn't a home that stifled; it was one that liberated. For Amelia, her home was not the end of her world but the beginning. A launchpad that catapulted her into public life, amplifying her voice in ways that still reverberate today.

Let's pause and reflect: What kind of legacy does such a home leave behind? When a house becomes more than a building and turns into a crucible where revolutionary ideals are forged, it transcends bricks and mortar. It becomes, as it did for Amelia and Dudley, a living monument to the enduring power of love, not as a social contract but as a pact of revolutionary coexistence. So, when we talk about Amelia Bloomer, remember the home from which she emerged daily — as a writer.

Chapter 6

Stirring the Pot of Social Change

Have you ever been in a situation where the room's atmosphere felt so thick with tension that you could practically slice it? Imagine Amelia Bloomer stepping into public life at a time when women doing so was an audacious act. But that room the collective American conscience of the 19th century — needed someone to cut through its dense atmosphere. Amelia was more than willing to wield the knife.

Ah, "The Lily." That newspaper she started from the comforts of her home wasn't just a pastime; it was a Trojan horse of radical ideas packed neatly between its pages. Initially intended to focus on temperance, the paper soon became a conduit for much more — women's suffrage, marital reforms, and dress reform. One can't help but wonder: Did Amelia realize that she was not just publishing a paper but shaping the narrative of a burgeoning women's movement?

With each issue, Amelia poked the beehive of social norms. You see, it was when women had little say outside their homes. Amelia made her voice echo in her home, through the printing press, and across the social fabric. Her words reflected her soul, scribed in ink but written in courage. She laid bare the societal inequities rotting in plain sight by merely speaking out. Isn't it fascinating how the most apparent truths often remain unspoken until someone dares to articulate them?

For Amelia, one of those glaring truths was the restrictive clothing that women had to endure. Oh, the corsets and petticoats! Symbols of feminine fragility and societal expectations. In writing about the alternative — a pair of loose trousers under a shortened dress, later dubbed "bloomers" — she wasn't just advocating for comfort but signalling a seismic shift in how women viewed themselves and their bodies. How do you wear freedom? Amelia had an answer.

But change is only embraced with resistance. The society Amelia challenged pushed back, and how could it not? People decried and insulted her, yet Amelia took these as badges of honour. Derision was merely the dying gasp of an old order resisting its inevitable end. For each issue of "The Lily" that she published, for each speech she gave in public halls, Amelia carved out a little more space for women in society. Isn't it intriguing how change happens? Not in sweeping acts but small, sustained increments accumulating into an irreversible tide.

Amelia's influence didn't stop at the pages of her publication or the walls of her home. In 1853, she took to the podium at the first-ever women's rights convention in Indiana, further solidifying her place in a movement that was catching fire. As she stood there, addressing a crowd on the ideas she'd penned in her home, did Amelia realize that her words were becoming the bricks and mortar of a new world?

Amelia and her husband, Dudley, actively participated in the Underground Railroad, aiding fugitive slaves in their journey to freedom. In doing this, Amelia clarified that her fight for equality was not just for women but for anyone stifled under the suffocating blanket of injustice. Isn't it telling how the fight for equality across one axis naturally extends to others?

Throughout her life, Amelia Bloomer remained a tireless advocate for her beliefs, adapting her views when they needed updating. She initially disapproved of the Civil War but changed her stance as she saw its potential for ending slavery. Isn't it refreshing to know that even trailblazers can course-correct?

But let's remember the community that Amelia helped foster. Her relationships with other suffragettes like Elizabeth Cady Stanton and Susan B. Anthony were not mere associations but symbiotic collaborations. They energized one another, each woman geared in a more giant social change machine. Picture that: a network of women connected not just by their shared plight but by the ink of Amelia's pen, the timbre of her voice, and the courage of her convictions.

The story of Amelia Bloomer is not simply one of a woman ahead of her time but of a person so utterly in tune with the essence of humanity that she transcended her era. Through her writings, speeches, and actions, Amelia shook the tree of societal norms so hard that it had no choice but to yield its outdated beliefs, allowing new, nourishing fruits to grow.

So, what is the legacy of a woman like Amelia Bloomer? It's more than a style of clothing or even a newspaper. It's a challenge to each of us: What are we doing to stir the pot of social change? Amelia's life whispers this question through the annals of history, and it's up to us how we choose to answer.

Encounters with Elizabeth Cady Stanton

Picture the meeting of two formidable minds, like when Edison first lit up a bulb or when Einstein scribbled down his theory of relativity. Sparks didn't just fly — they ignited an inferno. In Seneca Falls, New York, Amelia Bloomer met Elizabeth Cady Stanton, another fierce advocate for women's rights. Can you fathom the dynamism of that first conversation?

In Stanton, Amelia found more than just an ally. Here was a kindred spirit, someone whose convictions mirrored her own, someone who had also read the air and found it thick with the need for change. Their friendship wasn't just fortuitous but fateful. What do friendships like this do for the course of human history? They catalyze it.

Stanton was already making headlines with her unapologetically audacious demand for women's suffrage. Amelia, for her part, was propelling her ideas through her groundbreaking newspaper, "The Lily." Stanton's words on paper were like wildfire, quick to spread and consume old ideas. Amelia's writings, in contrast, were like a well-tended bonfire — persistent, warm, and inviting. Isn't it fascinating how two similar goals can be pursued through distinct yet complementary styles?

With time, their rapport deepened, their ideals intermingling as seamlessly as ink dissolves in water. They exchanged letters, each a capsule of thoughts and hopes for an unwritten future. Stanton inspired Amelia to question the physical trappings of women's inequality — the garments they were confined to.

Conversely, Amelia provided Stanton with a platform to express herself, to extend her voice beyond just speeches and open letters. Each offered the other something invaluable: a broader avenue to effect change. What happens when two driving forces converge? They don't cancel each other out; they multiply.

Ah, let's remember the collaborative editorials they worked on. Stanton often contributed articles to "The Lily," which Amelia would publish with utmost pride. These weren't just words on a page. They were revolutionary ideas presented to a public that was both scandalized and fascinated. Elizabeth's vivid descriptions of domestic hardships and calls for divorce reform resonated within the very framework of "The Lily," only to reverberate louder in the collective conscience. Isn't the power of shared advocacy astonishing?

Amelia Bloomer wasn't just content to stay behind the editor's desk — not when she had the chance to rally alongside Stanton. Amelia took her activism to the streets with her husband Dudley's unwavering support. Can you imagine the scene? Two women, standing shoulder to shoulder, holding signs that some considered heretical. Each appearance they made, whether together or separately, brought them ridicule and respect. The old order was cracking, and they were the wedge splitting it open. They were ridiculed, yes, but also heard. And being heard in a society that wanted you silent? That's a victory.

Though Amelia eventually moved west, their friendship survived the miles, and their advocacy continued in parallel lines that, while never meeting, seemed to stretch in the same infinite direction. When Amelia decided to pass the torch of "The Lily" to focus on her activism in Council Bluffs, Stanton was among the first she informed. Amelia's decision was met with Stanton's understanding and unwavering support — a testament to the nature of their friendship. Was Amelia's departure from the publishing world severing their shared mission? No. Instead, it was a branching out, an expansion. One less editor, perhaps, but one more soldier on the field.

Consider this: Some moments and relationships alter the course of history. The friendship between Amelia Bloomer and Elizabeth Cady Stanton was one of those pivotal junctions. Two lives, each extraordinary on its own, but together? Together, they weren't just a chapter in history but a turning point.

What does it say about the society they were up against that it took such monumental efforts to effect change? Let's turn that question on its head: What does it say about Amelia Bloomer and Elizabeth Cady Stanton that they took on society and left an indelible mark? Their legacy is of resistance and reform, built on friendship and mutual respect. And that, dear reader, is how you stir the pot of social change.

A Friendship with Susan B. Anthony

What do you think happens when destiny designs a meeting between two souls whose paths are steeped in the same righteous struggle? It was the year 1851 when Amelia Bloomer first encountered Susan B. Anthony. The setting couldn't have been more fitting: a convention for temperance. Ah, temperance — a word that, in that era, stood not just for moderation in alcohol consumption but also symbolized the changing attitudes about social vices and virtues. Amelia was already established as the founder and editor of "The Lily," and Susan? She was a young Quaker eager to make her mark in the world.

In Susan B. Anthony, Amelia found another companion, another fierce intellect wrapped in a cloak of unbreakable resolve. Anthony was more than a friend; she was a compatriot in a war that wasn't yet fully declared but had been silently waged for centuries. If Elizabeth Cady Stanton was the fire to Amelia's hearth, Susan B. Anthony was its cornerstone, providing a solid base upon which both could lean. What is the foundation, if not the silent strength upon which the entire structure depends?

Yet, their friendship was anything but silent. They exchanged pleasantries, strategies, ideas, and aspirations in private conversations and public forums. While Amelia wielded her pen as a sword in her editorial fortress, Anthony became a roving ambassador for their shared cause, her voice reaching corners of America still untouched by Bloomer's ink. Can you grasp the gravity of their collaboration? It was as if Amelia would sketch the blueprints, and Susan would construct the building — brick by laborious brick.

This friendship wasn't just mutual admiration but alchemy that transformed societal lead into gold. Take, for example, the famous "Bloomers." Amelia didn't invent them, but she popularized them through her paper. Anthony embraced this radical fashion statement in public, unafraid of the ridicule or the scorn it could, and did attract. In wearing Bloomers, Anthony was embodying Amelia's philosophy, her yearning for tangible freedom that began with freeing the body from its literal societal constraints. Isn't it symbolic of how a garment could echo a more prominent call for change?

The women faced challenges, yes, but they also faced them together. When Anthony decided to test the waters of public speaking, Amelia's unwavering support served as her anchor. And what do anchors do? They ground us while allowing us to drift just enough — to explore and discover. Amelia offered Susan her platform and endorsement, a validation that worked both ways. The duo shared the same lofty aims, yet each tackled them in her unique way. Amelia's approach was tempered and articulate, her every word considered; Susan's was visceral, almost aggressive, displaying raw, untamed passion. Different routes, same destination — don't these often make the best companionships?

Their friendship solidified over letters and shared efforts, was more than mere companionship. It was a partnership that transcended the personal to have a monumental societal impact. Both women understood the importance of communication channels. While Amelia thrived on the written word, Anthony utilized the spoken one. What would have happened if these avenues had remained segregated? The harmony between written and spoken word was essential in propagating their mutual goals.

It's true that Amelia eventually moved away, passing the torch of "The Lily" to focus on activism in her new community. Still, her friendship with Susan B. Anthony never dimmed. They continued to correspond, their letters a testimony to a time and a battle now etched in the annals of history. Is it not wondrous how the ink of a few letters could signify a commitment as vast as the sky?

We're examining here not merely friendship but a union of purpose. Amelia Bloomer and Susan B. Anthony were not just participants but flag bearers in the relentless march toward a more equitable society. Through articles, speeches, and the most elemental acts of rebellion, their friendship fostered a dialogue between two integral parts of the human soul: the desire for freedom and the imperative for collective betterment. This friendship didn't just add a footnote to the struggle for women's rights; it became its chapter.

Think about it. Amelia Bloomer and Susan B. Anthony, side by side in history, arm in arm in their quest. Two different paths, united in purpose and intent. Their friendship, far from being a simple alliance, was the coming together of two different worlds with one unchanging sky. A reminder that in the pursuit of justice, as in friendship, unity — and not uniformity — is the real strength.

The Growing Women's Rights Movement

Do you ever wonder how one person becomes the catalyst for something much more significant than themselves? Imagine a small-town editor — from the outskirts of American society in Seneca Falls, New York — joining forces with a broader movement that was beginning to stir the very roots of the nation. Amelia Bloomer wasn't just an observer of the growing women's rights movement; she was an active participant, a trailblazer, if you will.

Ah, the 1840s and 1850s, decades pulsating with change. Social and political currents were weaving a complex tapestry across America. Women like Elizabeth Cady Stanton had already fired the first shots of rebellion with events like the Seneca Falls Convention in 1848. Stanton ignited the spark, but what's a spark without a hearth to catch it? Amelia's publication, "The Lily," became that hearth. While it initially focused on temperance, it soon became a broader platform for women's issues. Why the transition? Because Amelia realized that the struggle against alcoholism was merely one thread in a complex web of female oppression.

Amelia's paper was unique for its time. In an era when women's voices were commonly filtered through men's perspectives, "The Lily" was by women and for women. The paper didn't just inform; it agitated, it educated, and above all, it inspired. In its pages, one could find discussions on property rights for women, educational reforms, and even marital laws. These weren't just whispers; they were loud, demanding voices that could not, and would not — be silenced.

Now, how did Amelia fit into all of this? She did more than just fit in; she stood out. A case in point — the Bloomer costume, the attire that caused so much uproar and debate. Amelia didn't invent it, but when she wrote about it and printed illustrations, suddenly, the outfit wasn't just a quirky fashion trend; it was a political statement. By embracing the Bloomer costume, Amelia challenged societal norms about how women should appear publicly. She wasn't just redefining fashion; she was helping to redefine femininity itself. You can't shake a tree without expecting a few leaves to fall, and they did. The conversations around the Bloomer costume ruffled enough feathers to stimulate even more public discourse about women's autonomy.

Amelia didn't just stop at her paper or her pants. She took her fight to the platforms that mattered. Alongside Elizabeth Cady Stanton and Susan B. Anthony, she attended and spoke at conventions and events, stretching her influence beyond the pages of "The Lily" and the borders of Seneca Falls. When Amelia spoke, her words were not mere sounds formed by the contours of her lips; they were echoes of collective frustrations and aspirations.

Let's remember Amelia's alliances in this journey. Her relationships with pivotal figures like Susan B. Anthony and Elizabeth Cady Stanton weren't just friendships; they were strategic partnerships that strengthened the very foundation of the women's rights movement. Think of it as a triangle, each point sharpening the other two. These friendships were mirrors and windows — reflecting shared goals and providing glimpses into different but complementary paths toward achieving them.

Of course, this era wasn't just about Amelia Bloomer or her famous friends. It was about collective action. But who rallies around ambiguity? People need symbols, something or someone tangible to stand behind. Amelia became one of these symbols. Her publication, activism, and even her fashion choices contributed to moulding a concrete form out of the abstract substance of female dissatisfaction. She offered a voice to the many yet voiceless women, catalyzing a societal metamorphosis that would impact not just her generation but those that followed.

The growing women's rights movement was like a rolling snowball, gathering mass and momentum as it advanced. It needed every hand, every push it could get. Amelia's involvement lent it velocity, yes, but also direction. Was she the only one? No. Was her role pivotal? Unquestionably so. Here lay a woman who seized the opportunities of her time and created them. She was a woman who saw her era's complexities not as an overwhelming labyrinth but as a challenging puzzle — a puzzle she was determined to solve, one piece at a time.

What do we see when we look back at Amelia Bloomer's role in the growing women's rights movement? We see a woman who was both a product and a producer of her time — a reflection of existing aspirations and an inspiration for future achievements. In a tapestry that was both intricate and robust, Amelia was an indispensable thread. She was a chapter no one could afford to skip in a collectively-authored story.

Chapter 7

Beyond Bloomers

When we consider Amelia Bloomer, what springs to mind? A defiant fashion trend, perhaps — a garment that ruffled as many feathers as the folds of fabric it was made of. But is that where Amelia's story ends, or even where it gains its most profound resonance? Far from it. The woman who gave her name to "Bloomers" was more than a style icon; she was a social reformer, a pioneer, a collaborator, and an influencer before the term was even coined.

When she moved to Seneca Falls, Amelia Bloomer didn't just enter a new chapter of her life but began writing a new book. At its core was her newspaper, "The Lily." Initially, it was a temperance paper aiming to slay the dragon of alcoholism that was burning through homes across America. Yet, much like Amelia herself, "The Lily" evolved. Soon, it blossomed into something more profound, advocating women's rights and suffrage.

It's fascinating how Amelia's advocacy transcended the written word. As it came to be known, the Bloomer costume wasn't just about shorter skirts and pantaloons; it was an emblem of greater freedoms. But here's the twist — Amelia saw this fashion statement as both a means to an end and an end in itself. Yes, the outfit was practical, but its true power lay in the conversations it sparked and the attitudes it helped recalibrate. Still, Amelia was wise enough to know that clothing wouldn't win women the vote or equal rights. That's why she eventually ceased promoting it when she felt it became more of a distraction than a catalyst for change. Isn't that the hallmark of a great leader, knowing when to shift focus for the greater good?

Amelia had a knack for networking — a crucial skill in an era when communication options were far from what we know today. For instance, her friendships with Elizabeth Cady Stanton and Susan B. Anthony weren't just about mutual support; these relationships created a force multiplier for their efforts. These were not friendships forged for Instagrammable moments; they were partnerships in the truest sense, each woman amplifying the others' messages.

Don't you find it intriguing how some individuals can skillfully navigate the complex terrain of alliances? In Amelia's case, these friendships also provided her with fresh perspectives. The transfer of ideas was mutual — Stanton and Anthony got a platform in "The Lily," and Amelia got firsthand insights into the legislative and societal challenges facing women. It was a symbiosis of intellect and intention, stitched together by the common thread of a shared cause.

Amelia Bloomer left an indelible mark on fashion, journalism, and social reform as the years passed. Her legacy isn't confined to the archives of her newspaper or the caricatures of women in billowing pants. Rather, Amelia's real legacy lies in the social shifts she helped instigate — ones that would ultimately contribute to granting women's suffrage in the 20th century. No small feat for a woman whose initial focus was advocating temperance.

When Amelia moved away from Seneca Falls in 1855, her departure wasn't a withdrawal but a repositioning. She continued her work in Ohio and later in Council Bluffs, Iowa. The geographical shift didn't dampen her zeal. Her activism took different forms speeches, writing, organizational work — but the core message remained consistent: equality. She remained active in community affairs and women's groups, forever the advocate.

It's easy to look back and slot Amelia Bloomer into neat categories: journalist, suffragist, fashion icon. But real lives, especially ones as layered as hers, resist such simplification. Amelia was all these things and more — a complex woman living through complex times. The bloomers may have faded from fashion, but Amelia's influence persisted, sewn into the fabric of a society that she helped to change, stitch by careful stitch.

So, what does Amelia Bloomer teach us? Isn't it that the world often remembers us for one thing when, in reality, we are layers upon layers of effort, dreams, and actions? Amelia's life wasn't defined by a single moment or movement but by a mosaic of them. And it's in this tapestry where her true significance lies, a significance that went far beyond bloomers.

Broadening the Lens: Suffrage and Temperance

What mental images are summoned when we conjure up the name Amelia Bloomer? Could we trivialize her legacy, reducing her to a sartorial pioneer with a hint of social activism? Ah, but therein lies the trap of historical myopia — Amelia's tale is not a quaint footnote but a seminal chapter in the women's rights movement. How did this figure, born Amelia Jenks in 1818, intersect so profoundly with the issues of suffrage and temperance?

Amelia's initial quest was singular: temperance as she took the editorial reins of "The Lily" in 1849. Remember, this was America in the throes of a developing industrial age. Alcoholism was a societal sickness, tearing families apart and wasting lives. To Amelia, temperance wasn't merely a question of individual morality but a linchpin in the crusade for a better society. Yet, temperance was the gateway, not the final destination of her advocacy.

How does a woman go from campaigning against alcohol to championing the right to vote? The answer lies in Amelia's nimble adaptability and keen understanding of the intersecting dynamics of social issues. "The Lily" began to navigate the broader ocean of women's rights. By the early 1850s, her editorial stance was unmistakable: women needed the vote.

Amelia saw voting as a form of empowerment beyond the ballot box. To vote is to be counted and acknowledged as an entity deserving of a say in shaping society. Women could influence laws and policy changes through voting, including those surrounding temperance. This interconnected view of suffrage and temperance seemed like a leap to some but not to Amelia Bloomer. For her, these issues were linked, like the roots and branches of a sturdy tree. If temperance was the tree's root, hidden but essential, voting was the branch, reaching out to touch the sky, the realm of greater possibilities.

It would be easy to categorize Amelia's work and see her as a journalist, women's rights advocate, or temperance campaigner. But the essence of her activism resided in the synergies she identified — the intersections of cause and consequence, disenfranchisement and despair. It's not that Amelia Bloomer left the temperance movement behind; she expanded the perimeter of her battles. The dynamism of her advocacy is evident in the pages of "The Lily," which carried debates on both suffrage and temperance until its last issue in 1853.

One cannot help but think about the courage it took for Amelia to push these socially charged agendas through a medium as powerful as a newspaper. This era was where women rarely had the chance to speak, much less lead. Amelia Bloomer didn't just find her voice in an unfriendly milieu; she raised it and, with it, the voices of countless women who read her work.

Let's not ignore the importance of the company Amelia kept — friendships with Elizabeth Cady Stanton and Susan B. Anthony among them. While their advocacy often received more public acclaim, Amelia was the linchpin who aligned different spheres of activism. She was the connector and the communicator, making voting a matter of public discourse when most wanted to keep it hidden behind parlours' closed doors.

Ultimately, Amelia's activism was not a frantic rush towards all directions but a carefully calculated expansion of naturally symbiotic causes. She once wrote, "It will not do to say that it is out of woman's sphere to assist in making laws, for if that were so, then it should be also out of her sphere to submit to them." A point that strikes at the heart of her ethos — an ethos not of duality but of unity in causes that aim to elevate the human condition.

To understand Amelia Bloomer solely through the prism of her namesake trousers would be a disservice. She was a force, a dynamo, an orchestrator of collective endeavours. She took the issues of her day, put them under a lens, and then broadened that lens to encompass a fuller, richer narrative of women's experiences.

Broaden your lens, and you'll see Amelia not as a chapter but as a volume in the evolving story of women's rights in America. And isn't that the essence of historical understanding — to look beyond the obvious, to probe and ponder until we see the multi-dimensional beings behind the names in our textbooks? Amelia Bloomer was one such name, a woman who understood the complexities of her time and acted, with unflinching clarity, to change them.

International Recognition

Amelia Bloomer — have you ever wondered how a name associated with an audacious clothing style for women became an emblem far beyond American borders? As we dive into this chapter, it's crucial to understand that geographic lines did not confine the reach of Amelia Bloomer's influence. Her work made ripples in the United States and stirred the global conversation on women's rights. How did a woman born in rural New York become an international figurehead in an age devoid of social media, instantaneous communication, and global news networks?

Picture Amelia, seated at her writing desk, the air fragrant with ink and parchment. She was drafting another edition of "The Lily," her ground-breaking newspaper. It was the early 1850s. Across the Atlantic, suffragettes in Britain were beginning to stir, seeking inspiration, tactics, and alliances. "The Lily" crossed oceans, each issue a small emissary from Seneca Falls to the British Isles and beyond. The British suffragettes read Amelia, discussed Amelia, and sometimes vehemently disagreed with Amelia. But most importantly, they listened to Amelia Bloomer.

Europe was a cauldron of social upheaval during the 19th century. Amelia's writings resonated with the European women fighting for their rights. In France, Germany, and the United Kingdom, her work was translated, discussed in literary salons, and cited in their burgeoning women's publications. What made her words so compelling? Her clarity — her ability to distil complex societal problems into an understandable narrative- spoke to the core of human dignity.

Amelia didn't merely talk about dress reform or temperance; she wove these threads into the larger fabric of female empowerment. While Americans like Elizabeth Cady Stanton and Susan B. Anthony were prominent contemporaries, Amelia had a knack for making the struggle for women's rights relatable. It was this universal appeal that garnered her international attention. Amelia was no ethnocentrist; her pen was dipped in the inkwell of universal truths, articulating a vision for all women, irrespective of nationality.

Yet, let's not mistake universalism for erasure of specificity. Amelia understood that every country had its unique challenges, customs, and cultural barriers that women faced. Thus, even as her writings found international acclaim, Amelia took pains to remain sensitive to the various dimensions of the global women's rights movement. She corresponded with social reformers worldwide, subtly modulating her messages to fit different cultural contexts without compromising her central tenets.

Why does this matter? Because Amelia Bloomer's international reach amplifies the essence of her work. Her influence wasn't the consequence of virality, as we'd understand it today, but of potency. Her ideas could traverse lands, languages, and cultural barriers. In doing so, Amelia Bloomer entered a rarefied realm of thinkers whose legacies become unbounded from their origins.

One mustn't underestimate the logistical marvel this was for its time. "The Lily" was not merely a product of the American printing press. It was an international document, disseminated through a network of ardent supporters who took it upon themselves to smuggle or ship it to eager readers beyond American shores. In an age when communication was an arduous task, the influence of Amelia Bloomer's writings abroad was nothing short of miraculous.

Her legacy wasn't built in a vacuum. It stood on the foundations of relationships, dialogue, and international sisterhood. Women worldwide felt a kinship with her, a kind of global sorority that traversed the limitations of time zones and geographies. It was through this communal struggle, led by women who had never met. Still, they knew each other so profoundly that Amelia's message gained an international hue.

So when you hear Amelia Bloomer's name, do not merely associate her with trousers or an American women's paper. Associate her with the worldwide stage of women's rights and reform. Recognize her as a pioneer whose language of equality was so universal it needed no translation and so nuanced it fit perfectly into different contexts.

Isn't it captivating how Amelia's words could travel thousands of miles, crossing physical and metaphorical boundaries? It's a testament to her messages' timelessness and a reminder that the struggle for equality knows no borders. In many ways, Amelia Bloomer did not just pen articles; she penned a movement, a call to action that resonated across countries and cultures. And that — that universal resonance is perhaps the most enduring testament to her incredible legacy.

Chapter 8

Public and Private Tribulations

Ah, the dualities of life — ever thought about how our heroes, our change-makers, carry a portfolio of public victories and private struggles? So did Amelia Bloomer. Let's temporarily strip away the sepia-toned halos history often places on its figures and delve into Amelia's real life, where accolades and advocacy danced with sorrows and setbacks.

We've seen Amelia on platforms and heard her voice through the ink of her pen, but have we considered what it cost her? Public life, particularly for a woman in the 19th century, was a tricky balancing act. On the one hand, Amelia needed to maintain an unblemished reputation, a currency without which her social activism would crumble. On the other hand, she was human, flesh and blood, with her vulnerabilities.

The strain started showing. Yes, it did. "The Lily" might have started as a temperance journal, but as it expanded to cover broader social issues, so did its scrutiny. Picture this: Letters flooded her office, ranging from effusive praise to venomous criticism. Amelia became a woman others felt they had the right to dissect publicly. Being a public figure, especially a female one advocating for change, meant Amelia's every move was scrutinized, her every word weighed for heresy or wisdom.

The private life of Amelia was no less challenging. She married Dexter Bloomer, an attorney and part owner of a local newspaper. Dexter was broadly supportive of her endeavours, but even within the four walls of her home, Amelia felt the limitations imposed upon women. Dexter's career often took precedence; the 'two-career family' concept was alien to their era. So, whenever Dexter's job called them to move, "The Lily" had to fold its petals and follow.

Why would a woman be so fierce and forward-thinking because Amelia was playing a long game? She knew that sacrifices were a necessary currency to pursue a better future. Sometimes, that meant putting "The Lily" on a brief hiatus or enduring a move that disrupted her network of supporters. Every setback was a step toward something more significant; every tribulation was a brick in the road toward reform.

The couple relocated to Council Bluffs, Iowa, in the late 1850s, drawn by the promise of opportunities in the rapidly developing west. Imagine starting over, rebuilding your platform and your social network in a completely different part of the country. Difficult? Undoubtedly. But Amelia was undeterred. Even in the face of these private and public tribulations, Amelia persisted. Council Bluffs became another theatre for her advocacy, another population to hear her voice.

Then came the trials of health. Amelia fell ill several times in an age without antibiotics or advanced medical facilities. Each illness wasn't just a personal struggle; it became a hiatus in her activism, a forced retreat from the reform battlefield. But even when bedridden, Amelia wrote, corresponded, and strategized.

It's as if her spirit refused to be caged by the limitations of her physical form.

The Bloomers had no children, a source of private grief that Amelia seldom discussed. The absence of offspring might have offered her greater freedom to pursue activism. Still, it also imposed a silence, a hollowness that the public could neither see nor understand. This lack of progeny weighed on her. Would her work endure? Who would carry the torch?

The capriciousness of public opinion, the gendered expectations within her marriage, and the constraints of her era — Amelia bore these with a stoic resolve. Each difficulty carried a lesson for her, and every storm cloud was a silver lining. Struggles were not obstacles but challenges to overcome, not hindrances but springboards for greater understanding and broader influence.

It's easy to look at Amelia's accomplishments and think her journey was an uninterrupted procession of victories. But the tapestry of her life was woven with threads of adversity as colourful and complex as those of triumph. Amelia's public and private tribulations didn't undermine her work; they informed, shaped, and drove it. They made her more human, relatable, and ultimately more effective as an advocate for change.

How we wrestle with our lesser-known battles defines us as much as how we handle our public successes. Amelia Bloomer, in her life's intricate dance of light and shadow, teaches us that truth with stunning clarity.

The Civil War Years

Ah, the Civil War — that great chasm in American history. It consumed lives, split families, and redefined freedom. But how did it ripple through the life of Amelia Bloomer, our pioneering editor and advocate for women's rights? It's an era that needs unpacking, not just for the broad strokes of battles and generals but for the intricate interplay of personal and political that it thrust upon individuals like Amelia.

Now, let's pause for a moment. What do you imagine Amelia doing when news of Fort Sumter came? With a nation at war, many would expect social reformers to pack up their placards and go home. That wasn't Amelia. She knew the stakes, not just for the enslaved but also for women. The societal earthquake caused by the war could either bury the women's movement or propel it to new heights. Amelia chose the latter path.

It's not like Amelia suddenly abandoned her causes; far from it. She maintained her editorial duties for "The Lily," though the war naturally began to seep into its pages. It's worth noting that the tenor of the journal shifted. Amelia had been cautious pre-war, threading a needle between audacity and acceptability. But with the eruption of conflict, caution felt like a garment too tight, too restrictive. "The Lily" began to speak more assertively, a voice attuned to the urgency of a country tearing itself apart.

Amelia wasn't one to stay behind her desk either. She went to work on the home front, participating in charitable activities and organizing aid for soldiers. But notice this: Amelia always retained sight of her overarching goals. Even in charitable pursuits, she argued for including women in higher roles rather than just as sideline helpers. Can you see her point? The war wasn't just a men's affair; it impacted everyone, and therefore, everyone should have a say in how aid was administered, how peace was attained, and how the future was built.

Amelia took issue with how the war impacted women, specifically. With men away fighting, women were stepping into previously forbidden roles. They were running farms, managing businesses, and becoming nurses. Progress, you say? Amelia would argue it was a false dawn, an allowance made under duress but ready to be revoked when men returned. What bothered her was the applause these women received for doing "men's work," as if these tasks were beyond their capabilities before. So, she used her platform to articulate this paradox: If women could do these jobs now, why couldn't they do them always?

The Civil War also brought a new focus to "The Lily"—the question of race. Amid a fight over slavery, it would be unconscionable to ignore the issue. Yet, it was a prickly subject in the women's movement, causing fractures that would take years to heal. Amelia, in her characteristic fashion, sought a nuanced position. She supported emancipation and urged her readers to consider how the subjugation of African Americans paralleled the restrictions placed on women. Yet, she was careful, perhaps overly, to navigate the intricacies of a society unready to grant full equality to either group.

Don't think Amelia escaped personal impact from the war, though. Her family was divided on the issue, causing emotional and ideological rifts that would never fully mend. Dexter Bloomer, her supportive but not wholly aligned husband, was also impacted by the war, adding another layer of complexity to their relationship. How do you balance the immediate concerns of a nation in crisis against long-term fights for equality and temperance? This question strained their marriage but also revealed its resilience. While Dexter and Amelia may not have seen eye to eye on every aspect, they remained committed to their shared ideals of progress and reform.

Amelia Bloomer's Civil War years, thus, stand as a pivotal chapter in her life. The era acted as a forge, heating her convictions to a white-hot intensity and reshaping her goals under the hammer blows of societal change. It provided a dramatic backdrop against which she refined her ideas, pushed her boundaries, and recognized the interconnectedness of freedom for enslaved people, women, and all. It was a crucible that tested her, as it did so many others, but from which she emerged more vital, more nuanced, and ever more determined.

So, that fiery storm, the Civil War, had Amelia Bloomer in its eye. She navigated it with a steely determination, altering her tactics but never her goal, which remained as fixed as the North Star: a just, equal, and free society. And through it all, she continued cultivating "The Lily," making sure its petals opened wider, its scent spread farther, even as the world around her convulsed. Amelia continued her journey toward that elusive but never-forgotten ideal through letters, editorials, and direct action. In this place, every individual could fully measure their capabilities. Wouldn't that be a world worth fighting for?

Chapter 9

The Thread of Social Reform

What propels a person not merely to live but to live meaningfully? For Amelia Bloomer, the answer to this existential question lay in an unwavering commitment to social reform. In every chapter of her life, social change wasn't merely an interest; it was the undercurrent, the defining melody to which she set her words and deeds. Yet, as any astute observer of history or human nature would agree, advocating for social change is complex. So, how did Amelia navigate the labyrinth of ideologies, pushback, and societal constraints that came with the territory?

Born Amelia Jenks in 1818, her youthful years were the breeding ground for a sense of justice that would guide her life's journey. In a world where women were often confined to domestic roles, young Amelia displayed an early appetite for education and betterment not just for herself but for women everywhere. She perceived inequity not as a fixed condition but as a challenge to be overcome, and this outlook would become her lodestar.

By the time she met and married Dexter Bloomer — a progressive-minded attorney and journalist — Amelia had already understood the pen's true strength. Together, they built a family and a partnership forged in the fires of mutual intellectual and social aspirations. Think of them as two pillars supporting the same tower of reform: sturdy, aligned, yet distinctly individual in their designs.

In 1849, as editor and publisher of "The Lily," Amelia Bloomer wielded her pen to tackle various issues, from temperance to women's suffrage. This wasn't a woman opening from the safe confines of her home but thrusting herself into the national conversation. She wasn't just a participant but a leader, a voice to be reckoned with. And let's not forget her bold endorsement of the bloomer costume — a modified version of the traditional dress worn by women. Deemed scandalous by many, it nonetheless ignited a debate about women's freedom to choose clothing. Who would have thought that fashion could be a pulpit for social reform?

As the years advanced and the backdrop of the Civil War painted America in shades of blood and struggle, Amelia's activism evolved but never waned. What happens to a reformer when the world around her is in chaos? Does she abandon her crusades and seek the safe harbour of neutrality? For Amelia, that was never an option. Even amidst the turbulence of the Civil War, she found opportunities to reach out to the marginalized, leveraging her editorial prowess to question the status quo.

In the Reconstruction era, her relocation to Council Bluffs, Iowa, wasn't a retreat but a recalibration, as she adapted her message to fit new challenges and audiences. The frontier West was an entirely different creature compared to the intellectual circles of the East. While many might have seen this as an obstacle, Amelia perceived it as an uncharted territory ripe for reform.

When you read Amelia's writings from these years, one thing becomes clear: the woman had an undying belief in the inherent goodness of people. She believed that most injustices sprung from ignorance rather than malice, and education could light the path to reform.

As Amelia and Dexter aged and their physical strength diminished, their resolve didn't. Their eyes may have dimmed, but their vision of a better society was as lucid as ever. The causes close to Amelia's heart began to transcend her, becoming issues that newer generations would pick up and carry forward.

So, when we trace the thread of social reform running through Amelia Bloomer's life, we find a string that's not just unbroken but strengthened at various points by experience, wisdom, and a tenacious spirit. In a world often resistant to change, Amelia stands as a compelling testament to the influence one person can wield when fueled by justice, equipped with the tools of intellect, and governed by the heart.

Was Amelia a product of her times, or were her times, in some significant way, a product of her? To pose such a question is to engage in a chicken-and-egg riddle, but the answer might be both. Amelia didn't merely exist; she lived in a manner that challenged everyone around her to live better. Her life was not just her own but a blueprint for those who believe that societies can, and should, always strive to be better versions of themselves.

That's the thread of social reform, ever-present and unwavering, that defined Amelia Bloomer. It's a thread that invites us all to pull, engage, and better not just ourselves but the very fabric of our society. And in that, Amelia's legacy endures, a resonant reminder that individual passion, married to collective action, can indeed shape the world.

Amelia's Role in Abolitionism

In a world teetering on the brink of seismic change, where did Amelia Bloomer position herself in the vexed issue of abolitionism? Would it be too much to say that her role as an abolitionist offers a crucial lens to understand the woman and the contours of a society in flux? The answer, as you might suspect, casts Amelia Bloomer as a vanguard of a moral imperative that would eventually reshape the American ethos: the quest to end the institution of slavery.

Born into the moral urgency of the early 19th century, Amelia knew from a young age that slavery was a wound festering at the heart of American society. But what can one woman do when faced with an institution so deeply ingrained, so universally justified by those in power? If you're Amelia Bloomer, you wield your pen like Excalibur and aim it straight at the dragon's heart.

Her husband, Dexter Bloomer — himself an advocate for abolition was not just a partner in matrimony but in shared idealism. Think about this moment: Here was a couple united by love and the quest for human dignity and equality. When Amelia took the reins of "The Lily," a newspaper initially founded to address temperance, she expanded its remit to confront the institution of slavery. She transformed her journalistic space into an anti-slavery platform, igniting conversations many wanted to shove under the carpet.

Imagine the resistance Amelia faced. Think about the societal norms and prejudices she was challenging. To her critics, she was an agitator, a troublemaker — but were these not the very terms thrown at all architects of change? Even some of her closest allies in the women's rights movement hesitated to bring abolition into their struggle, fearing it would dilute their message. Amelia faced a tricky line to walk — how to advance the cause of women while not disregarding the suffering of enslaved individuals? A less courageous person might have backed down or stayed silent. But silence was never Amelia's style.

What makes Amelia's role in abolitionism especially noteworthy is the timing. By the 1850s, the United States stood at the edge of the abyss, teetering towards the Civil War. At such a time, espousing abolitionist views was not just a moral stand but a political act fraught with personal and public dangers. Dexter and Amelia didn't just read about the tensions between the North and the South; they lived, breathed, and engaged with them through their writing and activism.

Of course, Amelia's voice was just one among many in the abolitionist chorus. Yet it was a voice that refused to be silenced, laced with an unyielding commitment to the core American ideals of liberty and equality. She was a vocal supporter of the Underground Railroad. She leveraged her influence to garner support for this life-saving network. The abolitionist writings she published in "The Lily" didn't merely echo within her immediate community; they reverberated, gaining resonance each time another person read them and began questioning the inhumane institution of slavery.

Isn't there something paradoxical about fighting for abolition while also being an advocate for women's rights? On the surface, the two causes would pull Amelia in different directions. But when you delve into the heart of what motivated her — the pursuit of human dignity and equality it becomes clear that these causes were not separate tracks but intertwined strands of the same ethical fabric she wove throughout her life.

As America bled and healed through the Civil War and the subsequent years of Reconstruction, Amelia continued to intertwine the causes of abolition and women's rights. After the Emancipation Proclamation, she did not sit back and celebrate a job well done; instead, she doubled down on her efforts to push for full civil rights for freedmen and women. It was as if she understood that the end of slavery was not an endpoint but a milestone on a longer road towards universal human rights.

So, how do we assess Amelia's role in the abolitionist movement? Was she the most famous or influential figure of her time? Perhaps not. But she was undeniably a vital thread in the intricate tapestry of social reform that defined 19th-century America. She was one of those rare individuals who did not merely reflect the struggles and aspirations of her era; she shaped them, challenged them, and, in so doing, left an indelible mark on the collective conscience of a nation.

For Amelia Bloomer, abolitionism wasn't an abstract concept debated in political halls or editorial columns; it was a moral crucible. Looking back on Amelia's abolitionist endeavours is to glimpse the soul of a woman fiercely committed to justice, who much like the nation she loved — was ever striving, ever faltering, but ultimately persevering in the long, arduous march toward a perfect union. And in that ceaseless quest, do we not see the finest attributes of not just Amelia but the evolving nation she so passionately believed could do better?

The Intersectionality of Bloomer's Causes

How do you stitch together the disparate threads of human suffering and longing and transform them into a coherent narrative of change? How do you navigate the labyrinth of issues as divergent as women's rights, temperance, and abolition without losing your way? If you're Amelia Bloomer, you don't see these causes as separate battles to be fought on isolated fronts. No, you see them as interconnected struggles in a grander war for human dignity and social justice.

From the vantage point of modernity, we often talk about intersectionality as if we've just discovered it. But Amelia was a master at weaving together different causes long before "intersectionality" entered our lexicon. The very nature of her activism was an embodiment of interconnected struggles. But why? What could link the fight for women's suffrage with the battle against the demon rum or the horror of human slavery?

In Amelia's life, temperance was the gateway to broader activism. The sin of alcoholism, as she saw it, not only eroded individual character but reinforced the systemic subjugation of women. When a man squandered his family's resources and abused his wife under alcohol's influence, was it not the societal norms that failed to stop him? And when a woman couldn't even vote to change those norms, wasn't she doubly victimized?

Then, consider abolition. On the surface, it might seem unrelated to women's rights or temperance. But Amelia saw the sinuous threads connecting them all. Suppose you believe in the sanctity of individual freedom. A society that allowed the ownership of one human being by another was fundamentally flawed and could never truly champion the rights of all its citizens, women included.

Her work in "The Lily" exemplified this symbiotic relationship between causes. It was a platform where articles on women's enfranchisement stood alongside scathing critiques of slavery. It was a space where the call for temperance echoed next to impassioned pleas to abolish the Fugitive Slave Act. This wasn't accidental; it was by design. Through the pages of "The Lily," Amelia demonstrated that fighting for one cause did not mean neglecting another. On the contrary, each cause strengthened and legitimized the other.

In marrying Dexter Bloomer, Amelia found a partner who shared her multi-pronged approach to social issues. He didn't just love her; he respected her mind and her commitment to social justice. Dexter's anti-slavery stance was a catalyst, not a backdrop, for Amelia's thinking. It was as though their marriage was a partnership in activism — their domestic harmony mirroring their shared conviction that temperance, women's rights, and abolition were inextricably linked.

How would Amelia respond to those who told her to pick a lane, to focus on a single cause? She'd probably say that life is interconnected, a mosaic of experiences that do not exist in silos. And true reform, the kind that permeates the very soul of a society comes when you address the rot in the system, not just the individual pieces that make it up.

In modern terms, Amelia was ahead of her time in embracing intersectionality, but let's not make the mistake of painting her as a 21st-century activist teleported into the 1800s. She was a product of her time, bubbling with contradictions and challenges. The crucible of these challenges forged her comprehensive outlook on social reform. When you're a woman born into a world that tries to limit you, when you're a human being appalled by the injustice around you, you don't have the luxury of fighting on just one front.

Amelia's life challenges us to see social justice not as a collection of isolated issues but as a complex, interwoven fabric of human rights and dignity. Whether she was arguing for the right of a woman to wear pants or for the abolition of slavery, Amelia's advocacy was always about much more than the issue at hand. It was about challenging the entire societal framework that made such injustices possible in the first place.

And so, we return to our initial question: How did Amelia manage to tread the complex labyrinth of social causes without losing her way? The answer is as simple as it is profound: she didn't see them as separate paths but as converging roads leading to the same ultimate destination — a just and equitable society. In the vast panorama of 19th-century American activism, Amelia Bloomer stands as a testament to the power of intersectional advocacy. She didn't just fight for causes; she fought for the concept that these causes could and should — uplift each other.

In that sense, Amelia Bloomer was not just a reformer but a visionary, an architect of interconnected change. And is that not the ultimate hallmark of any great activist — the ability to see the battle in front of you and the entire war and the contours of the world that could be?

Chapter 10

Bloomer on the Move

Do you ever wonder what it takes to be a trailblazer? It isn't just the breakthrough moments broadcasted or written down for posterity. More often, the dogged determination, the restless energy that says, "No, I won't be confined to the here and now." Amelia Bloomer understood this intrinsically. She wasn't content to let her feet gather dust, literally or metaphorically. This inherent restlessness — a constant craving for change and progress — marked Amelia's life.

Let's talk about Seneca Falls, the crucible of 19th-century American feminism. After all, Amelia arrived there in 1840 as Amelia Jenks, only to depart as Amelia Bloomer, a name soon to be synonymous with audacious reform. This young woman, then in her early twenties, had absorbed the values of social justice and activism from her previous environment. Still, it was in Seneca Falls that these values found a fertile ground to flourish. Dexter Bloomer, her husband, wasn't just the man she married; he was an extension of her aspirations, an abolitionist editor who understood the multifaceted nature of social reform. Their union wasn't merely romantic — it was a coalition.

In Seneca Falls, she entered the journalistic sphere by creating "The Lily," a temperance newspaper turned feminist mouthpiece. Amelia had the insight to pivot when the need arose. Temperance was a cause dear to her, but why stop there when the entire social fabric was askew? Here, in this quaint yet revolutionary town, Amelia deepened her ideological roots. She networked with Elizabeth Cady Stanton and Susan B. Anthony, women who would become not just friends but comrades in the march toward women's suffrage.

The year 1851 marked a turning point. Amelia adopted a style of clothing that defied convention — a pair of loose trousers hidden under a short skirt. These 'Bloomers,' as they would come to be known, weren't just a fashion statement; they were a manifesto stitched in fabric. Amelia said, "I refuse to be hampered by the constraints society imposes on me." But let's pause and think — why did a piece of clothing incite such uproar? Because, in an age that limited women to the domestic sphere, taking control of one's body was an act of quiet yet startling insubordination.

After Seneca Falls, Amelia and Dexter relocated to Council Bluffs, Iowa, in 1855. You might ask, why abandon the epicentre of feminist activism? Why move away when it seemed like her work had just begun? But Bloomer was not the kind of reformer who believed her reach should be tethered to a zip code. New landscapes meant new minds to influence. The couple continued their activism, with Amelia giving speeches and contributing to publications advocating women's rights, temperance, and abolition. The battle for a just society could not be fought solely in the drawing rooms and assemblies of Seneca Falls; it had to be a nationwide, even a global, endeavour.

In Council Bluffs, Amelia integrated herself into community life and resumed publication of "The Lily," extending its reach to issues like education reform. She became pivotal in establishing a library, proving that her feminism wasn't confined to voting alone. In her view, knowledge was the key to unlocking the shackles society had imposed on women. Her activism matured, taking on a nuanced perspective. It was no longer just about what women could gain but what society stood to lose if half its population remained oppressed.

Dexter Bloomer's death in 1881 could have been the bookend of Amelia's public life. Widowed and in her sixties, she had enough reason to withdraw from the public eye. But the fire within her refused to be extinguished. Amelia moved back to her native New York, taking up residence in her later years in the village of Lochland. It would be a simplification to say that she continued her activism; more aptly, she expanded the landscape of what activism could entail. She involved herself in civic life, proving that age could not wither her commitment to social reform.

Amelia Bloomer remained a beacon of constancy in her advocacy for a better world in a life characterized by ideological and geographical shifts. She was unafraid to pack her bags and take her ideas elsewhere to engage with fresh challenges and opportunities. From Seneca Falls to Council Bluffs and finally, back to New York, each move was not a mere change of address but a strategic repositioning. In the geography of social reform, Amelia Bloomer wasn't just a visitor; she was a cartographer, tracing the contour lines where the elevation of women's rights met the highlands of abolition and the rivers of temperance flowed into the ocean of human dignity.

And so, the restless energy of Amelia Bloomer echoes through history. Hers was not a life of idle contemplation but one of perpetual movement in both ideals and geography. She teaches us that being a trailblazer isn't just about the trails you've blazed; it's also about the courage to step onto new ones, machete in hand, eyes on the horizon, and a steadfast belief that a better world awaits. In her restlessness, Amelia found her purpose; in her movement, she found her mission. And in that ceaseless journey, we find the enduring legacy of a woman who refused to stand still.

Life in Council Bluffs

So, what propels a person to uproot life itself? Imagine leaving Seneca Falls, a bedrock of feminist activism, to strike out westward to Council Bluffs, Iowa. Seems like trading a fortress for a frontier. But for Amelia Bloomer, a fortress could also be a cage if it circumscribed her quest for sweeping societal change. Council Bluffs wasn't an escape; it was an expansion. It was 1855, the nation was simmering with pre-Civil War tension, and Amelia, the pioneer, recognized an entirely new terrain for activism. Could you think of a more calculated risk for a woman of her time?

In this Midwest town, she found a community still chiselling out its identity. Unshaped societal norms offered a blank canvas and fresh clay to mould. Her husband, Dexter Bloomer, became an editor for the local newspaper while Amelia continued her tireless work. Did you think a location change would slow her down? On the contrary, her activism acquired a new flavour. In Council Bluffs, her engagement took on a more variegated texture, expanding its contours to include issues like education reform and community building. She was the living embodiment of intersectionality before the term even existed.

Here, she encountered the grim spectre of frontier alcoholism. As a longstanding advocate for temperance, she saw this not just as a social problem but as a bedrock issue affecting family life, women's security, and community cohesion. The burden of her convictions found a natural outlet — speeches, articles, and community organizing. Amelia engaged with the world using the best weapon she knew: words.

Amelia resumed her journalistic endeavours in Council Bluffs, carrying the "The Lily" banner to these new western lands. This continued a conversation, an ongoing dialogue she had begun years earlier. But it was also a chance for new voices to join that conversation, voices that perhaps had never before contemplated the radical notion of women's suffrage or temperance. Who could be better suited for this task than Amelia, who'd been igniting discussions and setting conversational fields ablaze for years?

Education, that linchpin, wasn't to be ignored. Amelia worked assiduously to establish the town's first public library. Now, why is this significant? Because education for Amelia wasn't just about empowerment; it was liberation itself. A library was not merely a repository of books but a crucible where minds could be unshackled. The issue wasn't solely about gender or sobriety; it was about intellectual emancipation, connecting the dots between myriad causes in a tapestry of social reform.

Amelia also dabbled in politics — or perhaps it's more accurate to say politics were an inevitable magnet for her multifaceted activism. Her journey into the political arena wasn't about ego or ambition. It was a natural extension of her beliefs, another platform to argue for the policies she had long championed. She became an early member of the Iowa Woman Suffrage Association, tying the threads of her varied interests into a cohesive whole.

And consider this: Her life in Council Bluffs was more than the sum of her activist efforts. Dexter and Amelia were social animals deeply ingrained in the community. Their home was a hub, a refuge for thinkers, activists, and any soul who yearned for change. From the parlours of Seneca Falls to the frontiers of Council Bluffs, their household remained a sanctuary for enlightened thought and spirited debate.

A less committed individual might have considered this period a well-earned semi-retirement. But Amelia? She was building bridges, both literal and metaphorical. By leaving Council Bluffs decades later, she had turned a so-called 'retreat' into another frontline in the ongoing struggle for social justice.

In capturing Amelia's years in Council Bluffs, one can't help but marvel at her resilience. Here was a woman whose life seemed to be a series of moves, each a calculated step in advancing her causes. And it's tempting, isn't it, to think that maybe she was running — from obscurity, from the limitations imposed on her, or even from herself? But no, Amelia Bloomer was not running away. She was racing toward something, ever forward, a vector aimed at a future less constrained, more just, and far brighter than the world she had entered.

In Council Bluffs, Amelia Bloomer did more than live; she flourished, proving that the efficacy of a message lies not in where it is delivered but in its universal resonance. Far from fading into the Western landscape, Amelia leveraged her surroundings to amplify her voice, showing us all that the boundaries of activism are only as limited as we allow them to be. A fresh chapter in a storied life, Council Bluffs wasn't a detour but a testament to a relentless journey of advocacy and action. And in this chapter, as in every other, Amelia's voice echoed — not with a whisper, but with a clarion call.

Building a New Community

Imagine you're forging a path through an untouched forest — every step you take is into the unknown. You look back; your footprints are the only evidence that anyone has ever been there. Isn't that a vivid metaphor for Amelia Bloomer's experience in Council Bluffs, Iowa? Having moved from the bustling intellectual scene of Seneca Falls, New York, Amelia found herself in a landscape that was not just physically but also culturally underdeveloped. Yet, she was never one to see emptiness; where others perceived a vacuum, Amelia saw boundless space for creation.

Dexter Bloomer, Amelia's supportive husband, took up an editorial role at the local newspaper, turning the couple into one of the earliest influencers in the area. It was a position that granted him and, by extension, Amelia, a certain kind of power. A microphone to society, if you will. But for what purpose would they use this new-found influence? This wasn't just about promulgating ideas but erecting the foundations for a community enriched by those ideals.

Amelia plunged into Council Bluffs' civic life with gusto. The social fabric of this fledgling community was still on the loom, and Amelia became one of its most committed weavers. Public institutions — schools, libraries, social halls — were not merely buildings to her but the pillars on which a conscious, equitable community would stand. And isn't that what separates a mere dwelling place from a genuine community?

With unparalleled enthusiasm, Amelia worked to establish the first public library in the town. But a library, you see, is more than a house for books; it's a lighthouse for minds. Amelia knew that every book laid a step toward intellectual freedom and, in every educated mind, the promise of a more egalitarian society. She became a force for educational reform, driven by the belief that education had to be an accessible commodity, not a restricted privilege.

Her home, meanwhile, mirrored this community spirit. Amelia and Dexter hosted discussions that drew people from various walks of life. While their house had walls, their conversations did not. Every room was a forum where ideas were dissected and debated, where preconceptions met the guillotine, and where new understandings were born. And this was no echo chamber; Council Bluffs was a motley assortment of settlers, labourers, intellectuals, and drifters. Every conversation, therefore, was a microcosm of the community Amelia aimed to foster.

Social reform was not a single-lane road but an expansive highway with multiple paths. Amelia had a keen sense of this intersectionality. She extended her advocacy to the temperance movement, understanding how alcoholism was not merely a social but also a domestic issue, burdening women and corrupting the family structure. This effort wasn't isolated but synergized with her other causes, building a unified narrative for change. One must understand that every reform Amelia pursued was a brick in the grand structure of societal improvement she envisioned.

When we talk about community building, often there's an emphasis on physicality — skyscrapers, monuments, public spaces. Amelia, however, saw beyond the material. A true community, she believed, was an architecture of ideals built on the foundational blocks of equality, education, and mutual respect. While her husband edited newsprint, Amelia crafted social print, etching her ideologies onto the cultural landscape of Council Bluffs.

The Bloomers eventually left Council Bluffs, but their departure was far from the end; it was a graduation. The fledgling settlement they had entered grew into a thriving community under the tutelage of its self-appointed stewards. Even though they moved away, they left a part of themselves embedded in the town's foundations.

It's easy to see Amelia as a series of causes, a flicker of historical moments, or a set of stances and proclamations. Yet, isn't there a sublime beauty in recognizing her as a community builder? She wasn't merely changing a town; she was raising it, nurturing it like a child — teaching it how to walk, speak, and be.

Amelia Bloomer's life, especially her years in Council Bluffs, stands as a testament to what it means to build a community from the ground up. It tells us that communities are not just inherited but made, not just found but built. And sometimes, it takes just one person to turn a settlement into a society, a house into a home, a crowd into a community. Amelia's footprints in the unmarked terrain of Council Bluffs will perhaps fade with time, but the community she helped cultivate? That's an indelible mark; that's her everlasting legacy.

Chapter 11

Back to the Pen

Have you ever thought about the magic of the written word? How letters on a page can change the trajectory of an entire society, challenge norms, and rattle the foundations of convention? Amelia Bloomer understood that power keenly, and when she returned to her role as a writer and editor, it wasn't just to a desk or a piece of parchment. No, she returned to her armoury, armed with the pen — her weapon of choice.

By the time Amelia returned to the East Coast, the nation seemed to be in flux. The Civil War laid bare the divisions and contradictions lurking beneath America's veneer. While Council Bluffs had been a chapter of community building, this new epoch in her life was one of national introspection. The country was healing, but wounds of such magnitude require more than stitches and band-aids. What was needed was a radical reassessment, and who better to lead that charge than Amelia?

A ferocious commitment to the suffrage movement marked her renewed editorship. The War had concluded, but another battle loomed — the battle for women's right to vote. Amelia recognized that the moment was ripe; the nation was reconstructing, and what better time to question why half of its citizens were not afforded a voice in that reconstruction?

"The Lily," the paper she once edited, had folded by this time, but its spirit and indefatigable former editor lived on. Amelia contributed articles to various publications, and her writing imbued with a new sense of urgency. Her words were more than mere opinions; they were calls to arms. She wrote to rally, to invigorate, and to galvanize. Each article was like a stone thrown into a pond, creating ripples extending far beyond its impact point.

Amelia Bloomer was not just writing for her contemporaries but conversing with the future. She knew the seeds she sowed would not all bear fruit in her lifetime. And yet, she wrote with the clarity and vision that turned her ideas into inevitable conclusions. A woman's right to vote, education, and employment were not just plausible options for society; in Amelia's writing, they became moral imperatives.

The pen, for Amelia, was also a bridge — a way to connect with other leading figures of her time. Elizabeth Cady Stanton and Susan B. Anthony were more than just names on a masthead; they were co-conspirators in a grand project to redefine American womanhood. The correspondence between them was not trivial chit-chat. These were epistolary symposiums, debates on strategy and ideology, minutely dissecting every advance and setback in their shared causes.

In the years that followed, Amelia used her pen to challenge not just gender norms but also to confront the racial inequalities that persisted post-Civil War. It was an intersectional approach long before the term was coined. You could say Amelia was not just ahead of her time; she was ahead of many times, including, perhaps, our own.

The story of Amelia Bloomer does not end with the final articles she penned or the final letters she wrote to her comrades in her arms. No, her story persists every time someone reads her words and feels a sense of injustice at societal inequities; her gender does not determine every time a young woman recognizes her worth, and every time we, as a society, take a step — however small — toward the ideals she championed.

Amelia Bloomer died in 1894, but let's be clear: she never really left us. Her pen might have been set down, but the ink it spilt seeped into the fabric of American ideology, staining it with notions of fairness, equality, and the unyielding belief that we can — and must do better.

So, what do you think Amelia Bloomer would write about today? What would she say about our progress or lack thereof? Ah, but that's another chapter we're writing collectively, whether we realize it or not. In many ways, Amelia's pen is now in our hands. The question is different from what she would write but what we will. Will we be the custodians of her legacy, or will we be content to let her ink dry up, her pages yellow, and her vision fade into the annals of history? Ultimately, it's not just about Amelia's return to the pen but about how we pick up where she left off.

Later Writings and Publications

So, what happens when an advocate like Amelia Bloomer, who has already been at the forefront of change, gets her second wind? Is it more of the same, or do the years and the shifting societal landscape sharpen her focus, refine her insights, and intensify her fire?

When Amelia Bloomer returned to the role of writer and editor in her later years, it was as if she had never left. The paper and ink had missed her as much as she had missed them. Yet, the landscape she returned to differed profoundly from the one she had initially engaged with. Women's suffrage was no longer a radical notion discussed in hushed tones; it had become the loud rallying cry of women across America. And if you think Amelia was just about to take a back seat, well, you don't know Amelia.

The rebirth of her editorship came with a newer, fiercer kind of activism. The War was over, yet society was engaged in numerous battles: racial inequality, class struggle, and the elemental question of who gets a voice in democracy. Amelia had never been a one-issue woman. So, while voting remained at the top of her list, she also focused on these broader issues.

Her articles started featuring in various publications. There was no social media then, no trending hashtags; the power of the written word, inked on paper, mobilized people. Each of Amelia's articles was like an intricate puzzle, revealing a more vivid picture of social justice with every piece. As they circulated through reading circles, suffrage meetings, and private homes, her words started doing what they always did — ignite discussion and spark change.

We must remember that during this period, the feminist movement also grappled with the dangerous tentacles of racism. Many suffrage organizations were strictly for white women, a fact that deeply troubled Amelia. Taking an intersectional approach before "intersectional" was even a term, she used her platform to chastise the hypocrisy within the suffrage movement. She questioned, quite publicly, why white women fighting for their rights were willing to trample on the rights of Black women. That was Amelia — unafraid to point out uncomfortable truths, even if it meant alienating her contemporaries.

And what about her correspondence with fellow activists like Susan B. Anthony and Elizabeth Cady Stanton? These were not just pleasantries exchanged between old friends. Each letter was a repository of ideas, strategies, and sometimes disagreements. Amelia knew that these epistolary debates were shaping the movement's future direction. She respected the weight of each word she wrote, her position, and the critique she levied.

Here's the thing about Amelia: her pen was her sword, but it was also her compass — always pointing towards justice. As the years wore on, did she mellow, become complacent? Quite the opposite. The more entrenched the resistance, the more vigorous her writing became. Have you ever noticed how a deeply rooted tree is often the most resilient, its branches reaching skyward year after year? Amelia was like that tree, her impact growing exponentially over time.

It would be too simplistic to say that Amelia was just a product of her time. She was a shaper of them. Her later writings didn't just echo the sentiments of a bygone era; they reverberated through the decades, challenging us to look beyond our comfort zones. She wasn't a writer who happened to be an activist; she was an activist who used writing as her most effective tool.

Amelia's later writings remind us of the profound and lingering issues we have yet to resolve in a world still marred by inequality. She handed us a mirror, compelling us to examine our reflections. Her articles, correspondence, and relentless pursuit of justice still urge us to question our values, actions, and silence.

As the years passed and her hair turned grey, Amelia's passion never waned. With the fire of a young revolutionary and the wisdom of an elder stateswoman, she continued to wield her pen with skill and purpose. Amelia may have been born in a world that underestimated her, but she left it with words that could not be ignored.

Amelia Bloomer still speaks to us in many ways, her later writings whispering through the decades like a wind that refuses to die down. The question now is, are we willing to listen? And more importantly, what are we going to do about it? The pen, after all, is now in our hands.

Keeping the Torch Alive

Why do some people fade into the background as they age while others seem to grow more radiant and impactful? What sets Amelia Bloomer apart, transforming her from an activist into an icon? It wasn't about maintaining her ideals but invigorating them with time, infusing new energy as the world spun on its ever-changing axis.

Amelia didn't just linger in the suffrage movement; she helped redefine it, adapt it, and thrust it into a future she knew she might not live to see. The same woman who had championed dress reform in her early years now employed her advocacy skills for suffrage with seasoned tact. After all, she had the experience that only years can provide, along with the unfading zeal of a true crusader.

Her writings during this period became pillars of feminist ideology, those cornerstone texts that make you sit up and realize: "Yes, this is a person who understands the very essence of liberty and justice." As her life journey began to near its twilight, she took it upon herself to ensure the torch would not be extinguished. With the wisdom of years, Amelia knew that the struggle was far from over, and who better to prepare the next generation than someone who had weathered the storms herself?

She chose her words with the precision of an artisan, keenly aware that her essays would serve as guideposts for future leaders. Were her later articles a mere repetition of her early ideas? Far from it. As social and political landscapes changed, so did Amelia's focus. She addressed issues such as labour rights and racial discrimination with an eye on the intersectionality that would become a core element of modern feminism.

It wasn't merely her words on paper that kept the torch alive but how she engaged with her contemporaries and successors. Amelia became a mentor to many younger activists, sharing not just the wisdom but the how-tos: How to organize. How to articulate grievances. How to endure setbacks and capitalize on victories. In her correspondence with younger activists like Alice Paul and Lucy Burns, one can sense a passing of the baton. Still, it was more than a transition — a fusion of generations as if Amelia Bloomer said, "I've brought it this far. Now, it's your turn to run with it."

Remember, we're talking about a time when correspondence wasn't just an email you could dash off in a few seconds. Each letter was carefully composed, and each word was chosen to convey a specific sentiment or idea. Think of it as a painting — each brushstroke contributing to a more prominent masterpiece. These letters weren't just messages; they were Amelia's legacy, carefully crafted to serve a cause that would outlast her.

Then there were the public appearances. In her later years, Amelia stood before crowds not as a young reformer with radical ideas but as a revered figure. When she spoke, people listened not just because of what she was saying but because of who was saying it — a veteran, a pioneer, a woman who had seen it all, from the scornful sneers of sceptics to the uplifting cheers of like-minded souls.

But did the weight of her legend ever press down on her? Amelia didn't let it. Instead, she wielded her status like a weapon, using it to lend credence to the movement's newer, more radical voices. Imagine a leader secure enough to step aside and let the spotlight shine on others. That's Amelia for you. Leadership wasn't about ego; it was about cause and effect, about actions leading to outcomes.

The final chapters of Amelia Bloomer's life were a testament to the power of sustained activism. Far from being the swan song of an ancient idealist, they represented the acme of a lifetime spent fighting for social justice. She did not go gentle into that good night but roared until her last breath. The torch she carried, lit by her indomitable spirit, continues to blaze a trail for us today.

So, what does keeping the torch alive mean? For Amelia, it was more than just endurance; it was about evolution, about understanding that the true mark of a leader lies not in how they start a movement but in how they ensure its continuity. The world is littered with causes that burst into flames and quickly burn out. Amelia's cause, however, still burns brightly, a testament to a brilliant life. Are we willing to grab that torch and move forward? Amelia Bloomer has passed it on; what happens next is up to us.

Chapter 12

Diverging Roads

So, where do the roads diverge when you're already down the path less travelled? And what if that path is not just a metaphor but the very essence of your life's work? Amelia Bloomer understood this problem well. She found herself at a crossroads more than once in her journey, and each decision forked the road ahead into myriad possibilities.

It was the 1860s, a tumultuous period of American history marked by the Civil War and the mounting tension of social and political change. A woman like Amelia — dedicated, fiery, and pragmatic — had options, even if her time constraints framed them. She had made her name as a proponent for women's suffrage and dress reform, but the widening range of issues she began to tackle are often less acknowledged.

Human rights weren't a buffet where you could pick and choose the issues that appealed to you. For Amelia, these matters were interconnected, like a tapestry where each thread plays a crucial role in completing the picture. But let's not kid ourselves; there's a potential unravelling for every weaving of the tapestry. For Amelia, these diverging roads involved questions of what issues to bring into her already brimming platform, how deeply to involve herself in racial equality, and the evolving mechanisms of women's rights activism.

Imagine standing at that junction — every choice you make affects not only you but the legions of individuals who read your works, hear your public addresses, and correspond with you in ink that dries to form the text of history. The gravitas of such decisions wasn't lost on Amelia.

One significant divergence involved her publication, "The Lily." She had started it as a temperance journal. Still, it had grown into much more, addressing issues ranging from slavery to women's rights. But by the mid-1860s, Amelia discontinued her role as its editor. Why step back from something so impactful? She saw the changing currents — new voices in the feminist movement, the urgency of the abolitionist cause, and the impending sea changes in governance and civil liberties. The publication needed fresh energy and perspectives, and Amelia had the wisdom to see her role in its evolution had come to a phase of natural conclusion.

Another road forked when Amelia and her husband, Dexter, decided to move westward, eventually settling in Council Bluffs, Iowa. While the move might have seemed like stepping back from the epicentre of reform movements, it was a calculated decision. It opened the scope of her work to new terrains, literally and metaphorically. Amelia became an integral part of the suffrage movement in Iowa, proving that activism wasn't tied to geography. The fight for equality was everywhere.

Amelia's unerring ability to adapt is remarkable about these diverging roads. When she shifted focus from "The Lily," she didn't retreat into a quieter life; she redirected her energies, participating in the suffrage movement in Iowa and continuing to write for various platforms. This was no sidelining — a strategic manoeuvre in a long chess game where the stakes were nothing less than human dignity.

It's easy to lionize figures like Amelia, casting their lives in a monolithic narrative. But people are more complex than the history of the roles often assigned. Amelia's journey wasn't a straight path but a series of diverging roads, each selected with an understanding of its broader impact. Each choice was a complex calculation, a balancing act that navigated personal, societal, and existential considerations.

Amelia asked herself what was good for her at every juncture, but what was good for the movement, society, and the fundamental principles of equality and liberty? These weren't just principles inscribed on parchment or engraved in marble; they were the very fibre of her being.

So, as we traverse our diverging roads, it's worth remembering Amelia Bloomer not just as a figure of history but as a navigator of complexities. The roads we take may differ, but the essence of the journey — the why and the how of our choices — remains profoundly relevant. Amelia's life poses a challenge: When we arrive at our crossroads, will we possess the courage and the wisdom to choose the path that serves us and the greater good? In the tapestry of life, how will our threads contribute to the complete picture?

Amelia Bloomer's diverging roads weren't a sign of indecision or compromise. They were symbolic of a life lived in the service of manifold causes, each selected with meticulous care. While the roads diverged, they were all part of a more extensive journey — a journey she invited us all to join. Shall we?

The Waning Years of Activism

The arc of life is not a simple line, ascending steadily toward some peak of achievement and then tapering gently into twilight. Would it surprise you that Amelia Bloomer's life defied such geometric simplicities? Her activism didn't ebb as a mere function of age; instead, it transformed.

The late 1870s found Amelia and her husband, Dexter, comfortably ensconced in Council Bluffs, Iowa. The setting may have changed from the bustling intellectual salons of the East Coast, but the woman's energy had not. She had transplanted her advocacy, giving voice to the concerns of the women in her new community. Even as the years took their toll, Amelia remained relevant. Why? Because she recognized the need to evolve.

It was a calculated choice to narrow her focus. While the platform she stood on earlier had been vast — encompassing everything from temperance to abolition — she felt an urgency to hone in on women's suffrage. Why? One could say the impending reality of the 19th Amendment was part of it. But let's not underestimate the importance of wisdom gained through years of tireless activism. She understood that her voice would serve best when channelled into the key issues, especially as younger activists stepped into the arena.

Amelia knew she was part of an intergenerational dialogue. Others were picking up the threads she'd been weaving into the fabric of American society, fresh hands pulling them in new directions. Was she rendered irrelevant? Far from it! Her words, writings, and actions had helped set the stage for this new generation. In that, she found her new role — mentorship. In letters and through her continued writing, she engaged with younger women activists, providing encouragement and the grounded perspective of someone who had weathered the early storms of social change.

But what happens when an indomitable force encounters the immovable object of time? Despite her enthusiasm, her years began to register. She found herself less at rallies and more within the walls of her home, writing letters and articles. Her public appearances became fewer, but let me tell you, they lost none of their gravitas. Each appearance became a sort of cherished event — a rare but precious stone in the public discourse of the age.

And then there were the private reckonings. Amelia had long conversations with Dexter about the direction the country was heading. The machinery of activism could be all-encompassing, but so too were the quiet moments of reflection it allowed. What had been achieved? What was still out of reach?

The waning years of Amelia's activism were not an epilogue but a recalibration. It's tempting to think of the ageing activist in terms of diminishment. But that's too facile an approach, and it would be a disservice to Amelia's complexity. Instead, let's envision her as a wise elder in a vibrant, ever-changing community. She shifted from being the outspoken pioneer to someone who guarded the embers, ensuring they would ignite the next generation.

Only some get to see their life's work bear fruit. But Amelia did — she lived just long enough to witness the passage of the 19th Amendment. How poetic, how utterly fitting that she could see women gain the right to vote, a fight she had contributed to for decades. How many of us can say our lives have such bookends?

The waning years were Amelia's victory lap, though not one she took alone. For she knew that no triumph in social justice belongs to a single individual; it's the collective work of many hands, hands that she had helped guide and uplift.

So, as we consider Amelia Bloomer in the autumn of her years, let's not mistake the quiet for silence or the slowing for stopping. The river that was her life's passion might have flowed more gently, but it never ceased its forward motion. And that's the wisdom Amelia offers us even now: that the struggle does not end when we grow tired but continues anew, reshaped and carried on by those we've inspired. Are we listening?

Introspection and Retirement

Ah, retirement — that enigmatic phase of life where one is supposed to step back, ponder the vistas of a life well-lived, and rest. But what does retirement mean for someone who never really rested and found solace in the ceaseless work of breaking barriers? For Amelia Bloomer, retirement wasn't an end but a recalibration, a pivot to a different kind of involvement that combined personal introspection and a lingering touch on the issues close to her heart.

So why retreat from the spotlight when the women's rights struggle still raged? To understand Amelia's retreat into a quieter life, it's crucial to consider the nature of activism. It is work that consumes the soul. A constant push against the bulwark of societal norms. By the time Amelia reached what society would consider her 'twilight years,' she had already been through multiple lifetimes of intellectual combat. This phase was about choosing battles of a different kind — those fought within.

As Amelia transitioned to this new phase, her pen ceased moving. Oh, no. She continued to write, albeit less frequently, about temperance and suffrage. These eternal issues had sparked her soul as a young woman. But a new theme emerged in her correspondence with friends and confidants: introspection. Amelia pondered her choices, her lasting impact, and her mistakes. Who, in the sunset of life, wouldn't wonder about the roads not taken?

You see, Amelia began a reconciliation process, not just with the world but with herself. She revisited her relationship with the infamous "bloomer" costume, a piece of clothing she had championed and distanced herself from over the years. At this juncture, Amelia seemed to understand that her legacy was intricately tied to this piece of garment — like it or not. That reflection signalled a woman who had come to peace with her complexities. She understood that her influence had been symbolic and literal, woven into the fabric of the garments women chose to wear and the votes they'd someday cast.

Amelia's private life during these years was one of relative calm. She and her husband, Dexter, still resided in Council Bluffs, Iowa, a place far removed from the enthusiasm of the East Coast yet no less critical in the ongoing dialogues on human rights. Dexter supported her, as always, and they found contentment in simple things — books, the exchange of letters, and the warmth of home. Isn't that what we all seek eventually, the warmth of understanding and acceptance, first from others and ultimately from ourselves?

Interestingly, Amelia never saw the ratification of the 19th Amendment, which granted American women the right to vote. She passed away several years before this landmark achievement. But did Amelia sense it was coming? In her quiet moments of reflection, did she believe that the seeds she and her comrades had sown would eventually bear fruit?

To suggest that Amelia Bloomer "faded" into retirement would be a profound misunderstanding of this complex woman. She faded into nothing; instead, she ripened, matured, and acquired wisdom from years of battling windmills. What appears to be a retreat was an advance into the internal landscapes that every great reformer must explore to understand the why and the how of their life's work.

Amelia Bloomer's introspection in her later years wasn't an admission of defeat but rather a deepening of her convictions. It was a time for gathering the wisdom that can only come with age and distilling it into a form that would live on in her words, deeds, and the culture she helped to shape. If life so vividly lived could be reduced to its essence in the twilight years.

Amelia's essence was this: a fiery spirit that never ceased to question, push, and hope, even in the quiet of introspection and the solitude of retirement.

So, as we remember Amelia, let's not see her retirement as a closing chapter but as a well-earned pause, a gestation period for legacies yet to bloom. For aren't we all, in the grand narrative of life, looking for that pause, that moment to look back not in sorrow but in understanding? Amelia found it. And in doing so, she offers us the most valuable lesson — that a life in pursuit of justice is a life that never really retires. Shall we take a leaf from her book?

Chapter 13

A Wardrobe, A Legacy

Ah, clothing — that intricate fabric of self-expression. For some, it's just a swath of material to cover the body. Still, for Amelia Bloomer, clothing was a thesis in cotton and silk, an argument stitched into the folds and seams of women's attire. So, what exactly is the enduring legacy of the "Bloomer" costume? Can a mere set of garments encapsulate the fervour and complexity of a lifetime spent rallying for women's rights?

When Amelia first donned what would become known as the "Bloomer" costume, she didn't merely change her wardrobe; she flung a sartorial stone into the still waters of 19th-century gender norms. The ripples of that simple act continue to touch the shores of today's debates on gender and identity.

The costume — a pair of loose trousers hidden under a skirt — was revolutionary. Amelia made a statement that couldn't be ignored in adopting and promoting it. These were not just layers of cloth; they were layers of meaning. The trousers defied the notion that women were restricted to domestic roles. They allowed mobility — literal and figurative. Imagine how freeing it must have been to cast aside the weight of restrictive petticoats to move, breathe, and exist without the constant physical reminder of societal limitations.

While the public reception was a blend of fascination and scorn, the controversy amplified Amelia's broader aims. Each article she penned defending the costume and every public appearance she made wearing it resonated as acts of defiance. Yet Amelia was no fool; she recognized the symbolism, the potency, and yes, the limits of this garment. How could a pair of trousers match the weight of centuries of systemic inequality?

As Amelia's focus broadened to suffrage and temperance, her initial enthusiasm for the Bloomer costume waned. This was no casual abandonment but a recalibration. Amelia, ever the tactician, gauged the political climate. By the late 1850s, the "Bloomer" had become a caricature in the press, often ridiculed, sometimes denounced. Was she stepping back from the Bloomer to prevent it from overshadowing the more significant women's rights movement? Perhaps. Was she adapting her tactics, recognizing that the garment had served its purpose — to provoke, question, and rally?

Yet, Amelia would return to this pioneering ensemble in her later years — not physically, but metaphorically. Her articles and letters reveal a woman reconciling with her legacy. She no longer distanced herself from the garment that bore her name. Rather than getting rattled, she saw it as another way she was making a mark on American society. She understood that her influence had been direct and symbolic, much like the costume she had popularized.

Amelia Bloomer didn't live to see the fruits of her lifelong struggle — the ratification of the 19th Amendment granting women the right to vote. But she did live long enough to understand that her efforts, symbolized in part by that revolutionary wardrobe, were not in vain. How could they be when, decades later, the fight for gender equality would still be wearing the "Bloomers" of its time? Whether women wear pantsuits in professional settings or adopt androgynous styles as expressions of identity, the echo of Amelia's sartorial revolution remains loud and clear.

You see, a legacy is rarely a single, easily defined entity. For Amelia, it was a tapestry woven with activism, ink, and cloth threads. The "Bloomer" costume, whether Amelia liked it or not, is part of her complex narrative — a chapter in a book that refuses to end, written in fabric and ink, read and remembered by generations yet unborn.

Amelia knew well that clothes do more than adorn the body; they communicate ideas, establish norms, and even challenge systems. She may have worn the Bloomer costume for just a few years but wore its legacy for a lifetime. So, how can we genuinely gauge the influence of a life like this? By the ink of her pen? By the footsteps she took in those audacious pants? Or by the countless women who, knowingly or not, follow in her tread, pushing against the fabric of a society still very much in need of tailoring?

You see, it's all woven together in a garment that was never just a garment and a woman who was never just a woman. Amelia Bloomer, in her wisdom, became both seamstress and scribe, stitching her legacy into the very warp and weft of American history. Shall we wear it well?

The Sustained Symbolism of the Bloomer Costume

How does a piece of clothing transcend the cloth and thread that make it? The story of Amelia Bloomer can only be told by discussing the revolutionary garment that bears her name. While we may consider it a curious fashion choice, the Bloomer was much more than that. It was an emblem — yes, a political emblem — woven not just with fabric but also with audacity, ideology, and dreams of a better society.

Picture yourself, if you will, in a 19th-century drawing room. Women in layers of constricting skirts and corsets, unable to move freely, let alone engage in any physical activities deemed liberating. Now imagine Amelia Bloomer walking in, sporting her eponymous costume — a loose-fitting tunic over billowing trousers cinched at the ankle. Do you feel the room's atmosphere change? Can you sense the murmur that runs through the crowd? That murmur wasn't just about fabric; it was about something radically disruptive. The Bloomer wasn't just a costume but a manifestation of an idea, a sartorial testament to the women's rights movement.

Before you dismiss the Bloomer as a minor footnote in history, remember that clothing is often a visual shorthand for deeper social constructs. In the 1850s, the Bloomer became a symbol of the revolutionary women's rights movement. The garment was straightforward, practical, and untethered, much like the woman it represented. What better way for Amelia Bloomer to subvert societal norms than by stripping away the cumbersome attire that physically restrained women? What might seem like a minor fashion adjustment was a daring declaration of independence.

This disruption wasn't all smooth sailing — oh no. The Bloomer faced harsh criticism, even slander. Society was not ready to uncouple women from their petticoats so easily. Cartoonists had a field day lampooning women in bloomers. Religious figures bemoaned it as immodest, even immoral. Despite causing quite a stir, the outfit became the subject of everyone's conversations. Letters flowed into Amelia's newspaper, "The Lily," debating the merits and detriments of the Bloomer. These weren't just conversations about hemlines or fabrics but women's roles, rights, and autonomy.

But what of Amelia's thoughts on this garment? Interestingly, Bloomer herself eventually stopped wearing the costume that had caused such a stir, leading some to assume she had abandoned the cause, far from it. Amelia understood that the garment had served its purpose by disrupting the status quo and initiating a conversation about women's liberation. Bloomer knew that the dialogue needed to continue but evolve, that the movement was more significant than any one symbol — even if it bore her name.

Now, fast-forward to the modern age. These days, the clothes we wear say a lot more about us, not just as fashion statements but as declarations of the freedoms we hold dear. And yet, the Bloomer, both the woman and the costume, remains an enduring icon in the struggle for women's rights. It's as if Amelia Bloomer knew the costume would outlive its initial novelty to serve as a lasting image in the women's movement. When women today run marathons, climb mountains, or step into boardrooms in attire that lets them move freely, are they not echoing Amelia's original declaration of autonomy?

We talk of Amelia Bloomer in terms of her written work, activism, and collaborations with other great women of her time. But let us remember the Bloomer as one of her most powerful communication tools. Amelia's legacy is about more than just the bloomers that bear her name; it's deeply entangled in the ongoing fight for women's rights.

So the next time you see or think of the Bloomer, recognize it not just as a quirky fashion relic but as a symbol laden with a history of struggle, defiance, and an insatiable quest for equality. It's not just a piece of clothing; it's a banner that says: "Here stood a woman unafraid to challenge, question, lead." And if a pair of billowy trousers could provoke so much discourse, imagine what the woman wearing them was capable of.

Fashion as a Tool for Liberation

When we speak of Amelia Bloomer, the inclination to focus solely on the groundbreaking "Bloomer Costume" is almost reflexive. But why? What made these clothes more than just fabric, turning them into a lasting symbol of freedom? When Amelia appeared in that revolutionary get-up of loose-fitting pants under a shorter skirt, it wasn't a fleeting moment of sartorial audacity. It was a calculated move to unlock a form of freedom, one stitch at a time.

Now, consider the 19th-century American woman: she's nestled in layers of fabric, each serving a purpose, none serving her. Petticoats, corsets, and long, billowing skirts. Could she run? Barely. Could she engage meaningfully in public life or even comfortably execute daily chores? Need help. The clothing was, in essence, a cage, even if it was a cage wrought with lace and bows. Amelia knew this, and she knew it had to change.

The catalyst for that change was the Seneca Falls Convention of 1848. The first women's rights convention in the United States stirred something deep within Amelia. When she arrived, she ran into Elizabeth Cady Stanton, who had been loudly pushing women to adopt a more sensible way of dressing. But it was Amelia — with her knack for communicating ideas — brought the reform to a larger audience through her newspaper, "The Lily."

Think about the role of "The Lily" for a moment. Isn't it amazing that a little newspaper could shake society so much? It was here that Amelia made her stand. The message was clear: the fabric bound women was literal and metaphorical, and it was time to cut through both.

Amelia didn't invent the style she popularized; she adapted it. Elizabeth Smith Miller had initially donned the Turkish-inspired pants. But once Amelia adopted them, she became their most visible champion. Why? Because she understood something vital: fashion can be a powerful visual rhetoric. Each woman who stepped out in bloomers was, in essence, wearing her dissent, challenging societal norms simply by existing in public.

The bloomers, of course, met with backlash — caricatures, mockery, and denouncements from pulpits. Was Amelia surprised? Likely not. She was, after all, unsettling a societal cornerstone. The press accused her of immodesty, threatening society's very fabric. Ah, the irony! A fabric that was smothering half of that society.

Despite the controversy, or perhaps because of it, the bloomer costume served its purpose: it triggered a dialogue. While Amelia eventually stepped back from wearing bloomers, her departure was less a retreat than a pivot. She realized that although the bloomers were an excellent conversation starter, they were starting to overshadow other important issues like suffrage and temperance.

So why does the symbolism of the Bloomer endure even now? It's because Amelia leveraged fashion as a tool for liberation, crafting it into a visual vocabulary that even those who couldn't read could understand. It's a garment that declares a woman could be both feminine and free. It brought into the American consciousness the idea that women had the right to comfort, practicality, and, by extension, to public life.

Amelia Bloomer may have put away her famous trousers. Still, she never stopped fighting for the rights and freedoms those pants represented. Looking back, we see a fashion statement and a mission statement for women's liberation spelt out in fabric and thread.

In the pages of history, clothing might seem inconsequential. But through the lens of Amelia Bloomer, we realize it's anything but. The Bloomer was more than just fabric stitched together; it was a rallying cry, a declaration of intent, and the first stride on a long journey to equality. It's a real eye-opener, reminding us that choosing what to wear can significantly create change. Amelia knew this. Now, so do we.

Chapter 14

The Late Bloomer

What does it mean to bloom late in life? For Amelia Bloomer, the term carries an irony as rich as the fabric of the dresses she infamously defied. As decades accumulated, you'd think the fire of activism would dim, the spark of rebellion slowly fading away. But not for Amelia. If anything, her advancing years only fueled her lifelong quest for social reform.

In an era when age usually dictated retirement into the domestic sphere, especially for women, Amelia continued to challenge not just how a woman should dress but how she should think, act, and participate in society. The later years of her life got to the heart of her activism, showing how much it mattered in the grand scheme. She did not retire into obscurity; instead, Amelia Bloomer became more refined in her focus. Her activism wasn't a young woman's phase but a lifelong mission.

But what drove her to keep going? It may be the realization that while costumes change, the human condition evolves slower. The same injustices that propelled her early efforts still roamed the American landscape, albeit in different forms. And let's remember the continual progress of the causes she championed, however slow. Would you believe that some of the most potent validation came when she wasn't even looking for it? For example, the growing acceptance of bloomers in daily life reinforced Amelia's belief in the value of persistence.

Ah, the turn of the century — a time of significant social and technological change. Could a better backdrop exist for reflecting on a life immersed in transformation? Amelia lived long enough to see a new century dawn and the promise of even greater freedom for the women following her. For the reformer in Amelia, these advancements were both a victory and a call to arms. They signalled not an end but a transition, a passing of the torch to new generations of thinkers and doers. Yet, as always, the core of her message remained unchanged: the importance of empowering women to take control of their destinies.

One might wonder if Amelia Bloomer sensed the immensity of her impact as she navigated her later years. You see, she was not just advocating for the women of her time; she was shaping an ethos for the daughters and granddaughters of the future. The conversations she started transcended her lifespan, rippling into dialogues about gender roles, equality, and personal freedom that we are still having today. And that's the thing about late bloomers — they give the world the time it needs to catch up, proving that it's never too late to change the course of history.

Amelia's later years were not simply a gentle tapering off of earlier enthusiasms; they were a critical part of her lifelong arc, demonstrating that the fight for social justice is not the work of a moment but of a lifetime. "The Late Bloomer" isn't just a catchy title. It's a tribute to the enduring nature of Amelia Bloomer's ideals, a testament to the fact that true change-makers don't have an expiration date.

And so, Amelia Bloomer did not fade into the setting sun of her life without leaving an indelible mark. She didn't bow out; she blossomed. Isn't that what we all hope to achieve at the end of our journeys? To be a late bloomer is not to be late at all — it's to be timeless. And in this sense, Amelia Bloomer was forever in bloom.

Reflections on Longevity

Longevity is an intriguing puzzle, especially when examining a life as multi-layered as Amelia Bloomer's. What does it mean to have a long life in activism, mainly when each decade brings distinct challenges and changes? Living a long life isn't just about counting the years; it's also about how well you bounce back from challenges, adapt to new situations, and grow.

Take Amelia's activism, for instance. This wasn't a fad in her youth; it was the air she breathed, from the early days of her editorial ambitions in Seneca Falls to the societal battles she waged in the late 19th century. What kept this woman on her quest, who had already lived through more than half a century of struggle and transformation?

In many ways, Amelia Bloomer was a master of reinvention. Her editorship of "The Lily" allowed her to express the burgeoning ideas about feminism and women's suffrage. Even after she stopped writing, her influence didn't fade away. Her voice grew louder, encouraged by the growing chorus of women demanding change.

As the century turned, it was like a curtain lifted, revealing a new stage set with growing cities, emerging technologies, and a sea change in how people thought and lived. The younger Amelia, who once shocked the public with her "unladylike" adoption of bloomers, would hardly recognize the expansive playing field of activism the older Amelia navigated. Still, the core message never wavered: a tireless drive to fight for social justice and equal rights for women.

Let's remember the personal sacrifices. While her contemporaries began to retreat into the comfort of their domestic lives, Amelia Bloomer stayed on the frontline. It wasn't merely an option; it was a necessity. So, how do you keep that fire burning year after year without just getting worn out or losing hope? Was it sheer will? A deep-seated belief in the cause? Amelia's case has been a blend of both, fused with a certain kind of wisdom from living through decades of change.

The years might wear down the body but often sharpen the mind. And Amelia's long life allowed her to see — and contribute to — significant societal shifts. She observed firsthand the ripple effects of her early actions, whether the gradual acceptance of less restrictive women's clothing or the incremental steps toward granting women the right to vote. Such milestones didn't mark the end; they were merely chapters in an ongoing narrative.

What's remarkable about longevity is how it morphs our understanding of success and failure. Early setbacks, once agonizing, appear as mere bumps on a long road. And victories? They're sweet but waypoints on a journey that extends beyond one's own life. Amelia Bloomer must have felt this keenly as she moved through her later years, watching the new generation of women pick up the baton she and her contemporaries had carried for so long.

But here's where we confront the natural beauty of Amelia's longevity: the seamless weaving of her personal story into the larger tapestry of women's rights and social reform. Her life wasn't just a series of disconnected events but a cohesive narrative that spanned years, influencing and being influenced by the evolving world around her. Isn't that the hallmark of a life well-lived? To continuously adapt, to find relevance in every decade, and to leave a legacy long after you've turned the final page?

Longevity granted Amelia Bloomer a gift — the chance to see the early seeds of her efforts bloom into something much more significant than herself. She witnessed the beginning transformations of a society she had spent her life challenging, even if only in glimpses. And let's be clear: this isn't about mere survival; it's about active, meaningful, influential living. Amelia didn't just occupy a spot in history; she carved it out, cultivated it, and left it irrevocably changed.

So, as we reflect on the concept of longevity, we can't merely count the years of Amelia's life. No, we must also account for the breadth and depth of her influence — an influence that, thanks to the long arc of her existence, was felt by multiple generations. That's true longevity; it's less about the years in your life and more about the life in your years. In this vein, Amelia Bloomer remains an enduring example of how one life, well-lived, can echo through the ages.

The Turn of the Century

The turn of the century marks an epoch, a delineation between what was and what could be. For Amelia Bloomer, it wasn't just a temporal marker but a vantage point to view the vast landscape of societal transformation she had helped shape. But what happens when an activist like Amelia stands on the brink of a new century? Does she look forward with anticipation or backward with introspection? In Amelia's case, it's a bit of both.

While some saw the 20th century as an era of newfangled technology and industrial triumph, Amelia recognized it as a fertile ground for the seeds of social change she had diligently planted. Picture her then, the Amelia Bloomer who dared challenge Victorian norms with her fashion choices. Imagine her marvelling at the sight of women participating in the workforce, going to college, and becoming a vibrant part of public discourse. What had once been a whisper in Seneca Falls was now a cacophony of voices demanding change.

It's easy to romanticize such moments, but let's ground ourselves in reality for a minute. The turn of the century didn't magically resolve the issues Amelia had fought for; many remained as pressing as ever. Women still couldn't vote, and the spectre of inequality loomed large. But, and it's crucial to appreciate this, the battles had shifted from the fringes to the mainstream. This was no longer Amelia's fight alone; it had become America's struggle.

Amelia's activism during this era was far from ceremonial. She continued to write, giving lectures and contributing to publications. When you consider it, her lifelong mission seems to meld with who she is — like you can't separate the woman from the cause she championed. Isn't that the mark of true dedication? It isn't a passing interest but a lifelong commitment that bleeds into every facet of one's existence.

It's vital, though, to recognize Amelia's capacity for adaptation. The world of 1900 was not the world of 1848, and she knew it. She watched as the bicycle gave way to the automobile, as telegrams turned into telephone calls. Yet, her core principles remained unaltered. Amelia had that rare ability to evolve without losing her essence. She didn't just go along with how the world was; she rolled up her sleeves and moulded it into a place that looked more like what she had in mind.

During this transformative time, she saw a new generation of activists come to life — young women and men fired up by Amelia's work and her peers. There's a profound sense of legacy in that — realizing that the fight will continue long after you're gone. It's a double-edged sword, a mix of pride in progress and a tinge of regret for the remaining battles.

One can't help but wonder, did Amelia ever feel like a relic of a bygone era, even as she stood at the threshold of a new century? After all, the modes of activism were evolving, and younger faces were emerging as the vanguards of change. Yet, this is where Amelia's true brilliance comes into focus. Instead of fading away, she served as a link between what was and what could be. She welcomed the new century not as an end but as a new chapter, a fresh plot twist in a tale far from its conclusion.

So, as the 20th century dawned, Amelia Bloomer stood resolute. She wasn't a spectator in this grand theatre of social evolution; she was and would continue to be, one of its most eloquent scriptwriters. What she penned wasn't just a few fleeting lines but an enduring narrative that weaved its way through the tapestry of American history. And even as that century turned, bringing with it both progress and new challenges, the spirit of Amelia Bloomer endured, as indomitable as ever.

The turn of the century for Amelia wasn't just a calendar page or a chapter closing. It was a mirror reflecting both how far she had come and how far society still had to go. In that reflection, Amelia found her face and the faces of countless women whose lives she had touched and would continue to touch. That is the magic of standing at the cusp of a new era; you get a panoramic view of the road travelled and the endless possibilities. And for a visionary like Amelia, that vista was filled with the promise of a brighter, more equal future. Isn't that a cause worth standing up for?

Chapter 15

Women's Suffrage Triumph

The air was thick with anticipation on that summer day in 1920. Imagine, if you will, the quiet fervour in drawing rooms and the heated discussions in smoke-filled parlours. Across America, men and women alike waited for the final verdict. Would women finally gain the right to vote? For Amelia Bloomer, a woman who had spent her lifetime advocating for this moment, the stakes couldn't have been higher.

In the 1840s, when Amelia began her journey as a social reformer, the notion that women might one day vote was considered a whimsical fantasy at best. She had seen it all — the dismissive chuckles, the raised eyebrows, the scornful editorials. She had weathered them and ploughed forward, fueled by an unshakeable belief in gender equality. Do you know what it takes to hold onto a dream when the world insists you wake up? Amelia did.

The suffrage movement had come a long way since those early days. It had survived divisions, public derision, and political setbacks. Amelia had lived through those tumultuous years, although her active participation had dwindled due to age and health. She'd watched younger activists like Alice Paul and Carrie Chapman Catt take up the mantle, adding new tactics and zest to a cause Amelia had championed when bloomers were still considered outrageous. And now, here it was — the movement standing on the precipice of a historic breakthrough.

Let's pause for a second to consider the fate. Amelia breathed life into the early women's movement through her writings and wardrobe rebellion. Yet, a generation later, long after her active years had waned, this monumental change was on the cusp of happening. Was it chance or destiny that Amelia lived just long enough to witness the 19th Amendment's ratification?

For Amelia, however, the triumph was bittersweet. Her eyes, those windows to a soul that had seen so much, also saw friends and fellow warriors like Elizabeth Cady Stanton and Susan B. Anthony depart this world without casting a vote. They had fought the good fight and laid the groundwork but wouldn't be there to walk into a voting booth. How does one celebrate a victory that has come too late for some of those most dear?

Amelia would only live a short time to participate extensively in the political process she had helped pioneer. She died in 1894, well before women in every state could step into a voting booth. Still, her influence in the triumph was indelible. For it was Amelia who had often provided the intellectual fodder for the movement through her publication, "The Lily." She had given women the initial courage to question, reject the patriarchal norms, and aspire for something greater.

Her battle wasn't just about the ballot; it was a crusade for the dignity and worth of half the population. It asserted that women should have a say in the matters that governed their lives — from the laws passed to the politicians who passed them. In August 1920, when the 19th Amendment was ratified, Amelia's dreams and those of countless women she inspired became part of America's reality.

Don't you find it poetic? The story of Amelia Bloomer converges with the triumphant crescendo of women's suffrage, like a melody meeting its perfect final note. If Amelia could have been there, ballot in hand, one could imagine her filling in the circle with a sense of satisfaction, perhaps even whispering a quiet "thank you" to all those who had come before and would come after.

As you turn this page, understand that the triumph of the 19th Amendment wasn't just the end of a long struggle and the beginning of a new era. Amelia had glimpsed an era in her boldest dreams where little girls could grow up knowing their voice had weight; their choices had consequences, and their potential limitless.

In this chapter, we don't merely celebrate a historical milestone. We acknowledge the tenacity and spirit of Amelia Bloomer, whose work transcended her lifetime to become a cornerstone of women's liberation. Although Amelia was not there to cast a vote, her spirit was undoubtedly present, and it is that spirit that continues to shape and fuel the quest for gender equality today.

What about you, dear reader? As you reflect on this triumph, ask yourself what causes are worth your advocacy, your time, and perhaps even a tiny rebellion. After all, Amelia Bloomer showed us that the pursuit of justice, no matter how long it takes, is always a fight worth engaging in.

The Victory of the 19th Amendment

Ah, the 19th Amendment — a crowning achievement for women's rights in the United States and would be synonymous with Amelia Bloomer, albeit posthumously. How did we get to this point where women finally earned their rightful place in the democratic fabric of America? Amelia paved the path for this monumental event in her unique way.

By the time the 19th Amendment was ratified on August 18, 1920, Amelia had been gone for almost three decades. Yet, her spirit must have hovered around those who rejoiced. Do you ever think about how legacies ripple through time? How do they grow stronger with each soul they touch? That's the kind of legacy Amelia had crafted, one that championed the voiceless and demanded equality for women.

There was something raw about the world Amelia had entered when she first started her journey toward social reform. Women were taught to be the "Angels of the House," their voices silenced by the echo of male opinions. Women had no say in legislation, no right to property, and were often denied access to education. It was a stage set for complacency, yet Amelia would have none of it. In stepping onto that stage, she sparked a dialogue that would ultimately result in the 19th Amendment.

Amelia Bloomer's innovative spirit wasn't limited to her Bloomer costume; it permeated into her editorial endeavours as well. With "The Lily," she moved the needle, speaking on the unspeakable — women's rights and suffrage. "The Lily" was a springboard for other feminist thinkers like Elizabeth Cady Stanton and Susan B. Anthony. Amelia introduced the two women, unknowingly setting the stage for a friendship to propel the women's suffrage movement forward.

What made Amelia such an effective advocate? Sure, she had a pen mightier than most, but her ability to catalyze conversations mattered. Conversations that questioned — and often shattered — the status quo. Isn't that the essence of any revolution?

Dudley Bloomer, Amelia's husband, once said that Amelia "was not a woman to be passively content." Neither were the women she inspired. Stanton and Anthony founded the National Woman Suffrage Association, which advocated for a constitutional amendment allowing women to vote. This struggle continued for decades, shaping and reshaping the nation's destiny.

Yes, Amelia was no longer physically present to witness the victory of the 19th Amendment. Still, it's hard to believe her influence wasn't felt. We often measure life by its length, but Amelia's life speaks to the width and depth of existence, not just the years lived. Would Stanton and Anthony have been as effective without Amelia's early influence? Perhaps. But there's a unique kind of power in being the catalyst, in setting the first dominos in motion.

The ratification of the 19th Amendment was far from the end of the journey for women's rights. Yet, it serves as a landmark, a checkpoint that screams progress. It symbolizes the battles fought and won, the endless orations, and the ink spilt in editorial columns — all merging into a moment of triumph. A triumph, Amelia might say, that was long overdue.

While critics would later argue about the limitations of the Amendment — that it largely benefitted white women and ignored the intersectional complications faced by women of colour — the significance of its ratification cannot be negated. The 19th Amendment is a testament to the fortitude of countless women who, inspired by pioneers like Amelia Bloomer, refused to be muted. It symbolized validation, the nation admitting that women deserve their say, too.

Amelia's legacy didn't just end with her passing; it evolved. The 19th Amendment and all it encapsulates was like a love letter to the activism Amelia embodied. It was a victory that took root in her unconventional perspectives, sprouted through her journalism, and flowered in her ceaseless activism. The Amendment serves as a reminder that Amelia Bloomer and the women she inspired had — in fact — changed the world.

Can a legacy honestly be forgotten if its impact remains woven into the very fabric of society? Amelia's principles continue to manifest in each electoral ballot cast by a woman, each political office held by a woman, and each law passed that nudges us closer to gender equality.

What would Amelia think of this world today, where women not only vote but also run corporations, govern states, and shape policies? We can only speculate. But one thing remains clear: the victory of the 19th Amendment was a culmination of tireless advocacy sparked by the likes of Amelia Bloomer. And so, even though she never cast a vote, every ballot paper now filled by a woman bears her invisible fingerprint.

Amelia's Posthumous Impact

What does it mean to endure? What does it mean for your legacy to defy the relentless march of time? For Amelia Bloomer, a woman born in an era where her gender was a boundary, the passage of time has only made her legacy more resonant. Do we still need to battle societal norms, fighting for equal footing in public and private spheres alike? Amelia, your voice rings clear even today.

The durability of Amelia's legacy defies a simple explanation. But, perhaps the very complexity of this woman — an amalgamation of editor, fashion rebel, social activist, and suffragist — accounts for her timeless relevance. Her name may forever be linked to a clothing style, but the bloomers were always more than fabric and stitches. No, they were a vivid metaphor for challenging the constrictive norms of a society that had long subjugated women.

Now, take a moment and consider: How many women have walked into polling stations unaccompanied, standing tall and filled with purpose, utterly oblivious to the battles fought for this simple act? The 19th Amendment, the landmark achievement that finally granted American women the right to vote, arrived decades after Amelia's demise. Yet the ink that flowed from her pen, the words she scribed in "The Lily," seeped into the fabric of this long struggle. Even though she couldn't cast a ballot herself, Amelia contributed to shaping a society that would eventually allow her spiritual daughters to do so.

Amelia's journalistic endeavours offered more than a soapbox for her causes; they created a space where like-minded souls could gather. Imagine the hunger in the eyes of a young woman in 1853 as she read an issue of The Lily. Picture her feeling seen, maybe for the first time. Now, transpose that scene to the modern age, where a young activist stumbles upon Amelia's writings online. Across the gulfs of time and technology, the connection remains unbroken.

And what about the advocates for gender equality today? Elizabeth Cady Stanton Susan B. Anthony, known to most as a foundational figure in women's rights, had a less documented but intensely significant companion in Amelia. Her initial platform gave voice to Stanton, and her life's work became a thread intricately woven into the quilt of the suffrage movement, one that continued to unfurl long after she was gone.

But Amelia was not a one-note character; she was a multifaceted individual with convictions extending beyond suffrage and bloomers. Her advocacy for temperance and her dalliances with abolitionism placed her at the intersections of the most significant social debates of her time — debates we echo in our era. Where would the conversations on intersectional feminism be without Amelia's pioneering stance?

But of course, even enduring legacies face periods of erosion. There were decades — even when Amelia Bloomer's name elicited little more than historical footnotes or superficial mentions in fashion chronicles. That's the irony of being ahead of your time: sometimes, the world must catch up to fully appreciate the trail you've blazed.

And catch up, it did. Amelia's life and contributions are subjects of fresh scholarly work. At the same time, the issues she championed have found renewed vigour in 21st-century dialogues. The garments that once scandalized a nation have evolved and been reinterpreted by contemporary designers as an emblem of feminist liberation. Amelia's echo in modern discourse may be a whisper compared to the roars of her contemporaries. Still, even a whisper can be powerful when it speaks undeniable truths.

Ultimately, Amelia Bloomer remains a figure of her time and timeless. Her voice, amplified by ink and paper, friendship and advocacy, fashion and defiance, still reverberates. To remember her merely as the namesake of a garment would be to misunderstand the expansiveness of her impact. Amelia didn't just live in history; she helped create it. In doing so, she also shaped a future she would never see — a future where every little girl could grow up believing she, too, could stir the pot of social change.

So, as we push forward in our battles, wrestling with social constructs and legal limitations, let's pause to nod in gratitude to Amelia Bloomer. The ink of her pen may have long dried, but its indelible mark on the fight for gender equality lives on. No, Amelia, you have not faded into history; you have etched yourself into its core.

Chapter 16

Controversies and Criticisms

Who was Amelia Bloomer? A feminist? A revolutionary? An agitator? The accolades she garnered during her lifetime and the posthumous adoration that showered upon her memory make it easy to forget: not everyone agreed with Amelia Bloomer. But isn't that the essence of a revolutionary — to disrupt, challenge, and make some uncomfortable?

In Amelia's life, the costume that bore her name generated more than just headlines; it unleashed a fury of criticism. Newspapers had a field day lampooned women who donned "bloomers," as they quickly became known. Society questioned: Could a woman advocating for such a departure from traditional femininity be trusted with any measure of seriousness? To some, Amelia's bloomers seemed not just a fashion statement but a slap in the face of conventional mores. To the critics, she was attempting to dissolve the very fibres of American society. Yet, the bloomers were never merely about fabric or style; at their core, they were a cry against confinements — of garments and roles.

Now, consider the realm of journalism. Amelia's venture into publishing "The Lily" was groundbreaking, yes, but not universally praised. Some of her male contemporaries questioned the appropriateness of a woman taking the pen to discuss issues like politics and social reform. After all, the 19th-century press was a male-dominated sphere, and Amelia was pushing the boundaries. Was she too assertive, too loud, too disruptive? These questions followed her, but for Amelia, the criticisms were embers that fueled the fire within her.

Amelia found a supportive sisterhood in her friendship and correspondence with other women's rights advocates like Susan B. Anthony and Elizabeth Cady Stanton. But even here, controversies thrived. Amelia was often sandwiched between differing ideologies and strategies within the women's rights movement. Debates over whether to pursue the right to vote aggressively or focus on more "acceptable" issues like temperance splintered the community. Amelia navigated these diverging roads with care but not without drawing criticism from both sides.

Beyond the borders of the United States, Amelia received international attention. While some in Europe lauded her efforts, others saw her as an exemplar of "loose American morals." Imagine that — standing as a singular representative for the morality, or lack thereof, of an entire nation!

Now, let's pivot. What happens when we examine Amelia through modern lenses? The history study often involves reevaluating heroes, and Amelia is no exception. Modern scholars have questioned the limited scope of her feminism, mainly its focus primarily on the concerns of white, middle-class women. The spectre of 'white feminism' hovers over her legacy. Although this criticism must be contextualized within the constraints of her time, it remains a part of the complex tapestry that is Amelia Bloomer.

What about the arguments that her journalistic style — assertive, direct, unyielding — excluded those who could have been allies? In today's parlance, was Amelia Bloomer too divisive? This question also tugs at the coattails of her legacy. Yet, one could argue that Amelia's uncompromising stance was the catalyst that propelled women's rights issues into the public discourse.

Amelia's life was a tableau of inspiring triumphs and harsh criticisms. The controversies that swirled around her did not define her, but they did shape the way she was perceived by her contemporaries and how we, in turn, remember her today. And it's precisely because she was controversial that she was transformative.

In reckoning with Amelia Bloomer, we confront the tension surrounding pioneers — those who stretch societal boundaries are inevitably met with resistance. It's a form of societal checks and balances. A dialogue between tradition and progress. And in that dialogue, Amelia's voice was unmistakable. Loud, yes. Controversial, without a doubt. But also indispensable.

Criticism and controversy are not mere footnotes in Amelia's biography; they are chapters in a life rich with complexity and a legacy resonant with impact. So, as we peel back the layers of her life, we discover that Amelia Bloomer was neither a saint nor a villain. She was intensely human, full of contradictions and complexities that made her compelling. And maybe that's why we're still talking about her today.

Facing Opposition: Both Then and Now

Is there a price to pay for being ahead of your time? If you asked Amelia Bloomer, she'd say yes. Still, the cost — measured in scorn and ridicule — was well worth the progress that could be ignited. It's essential, though, to consider Amelia's life not merely as an antecedent for our modern discussions but within the framework of the fiery debates and fervent opposition she encountered in her lifetime.

The notion of a woman stepping into the realm of activism during Amelia's era was about as fitting, in the eyes of many, as a square peg in a round hole. These were times when women were expected to exist within the domestic sphere — cooking, cleaning, nurturing. And here was Amelia, with her audacious pants and rebellious ink, effectively shaking the societal snow globe.

Beneath the voluminous layers of her unconventional garments, Amelia carried the weight of public scrutiny. Let's not forget — bloomers were more than mere pieces of fabric; they were seen as direct challenges to the established norms of femininity. Critics argued that Amelia and her fashion-forward followers attempted to assume men's roles and appearances. Could these women, who dared to defy the established norms of fashion, be trusted with anything more serious? This was a legitimate query in the social discourse of the time. To the most vocal critics, Amelia's garments became symbols of chaos and disorder, as if wearing pants could unravel the very fabric of society.

Let's step into the realm of print media. When Amelia published The Lily, her choice of topics — suffrage, temperance, equality — rattled the status quo. Detractors weren't just men clinging to patriarchal benefits; some were women who believed that activism should remain a male prerogative. These opposing voices claimed that Amelia was upending the natural order. Still, they failed to see the underlying philosophy of her actions: the audacity to imagine a world where women had equal standing.

And then there were the tensions within the activist circles. Sometimes, the sharpest barbs come from your side of the fence. Amelia was caught in the crossfire between suffragists who wanted to charge full-throttle at the voting issue and others who advocated for a more gradual approach. Either way, her role was dissected, and her strategies were questioned.

Fast forward to the present day. How do modern critics see Amelia Bloomer? Revisionist historians have brought up valid points, emphasizing the limitations of her activism — mainly its focus on white, middle-class women. While such an observation is anachronistic, applying today's standards of intersectionality to a 19th-century context brings a necessary nuance to our understanding of her.

And here we have it — the cycle of opposition that seems to spin eternally. Even in today's climate, some corners question whether Amelia deserves her place in the feminist canon. They ask, was she too narrow in her focus? Too insistent in her voice? As we scrutinize Amelia through the lens of modernity, it's apparent that challenges to her legacy persist.

To understand Amelia is to grasp the essence of opposition itself. She was the epitome of a disruptor, a role that naturally invites confrontation. Whether facing off against societal norms or contending with differing ideologies within her movement, Amelia's life was steeped in opposition. This wasn't a footnote; it was an ongoing narrative.

Does the opposition, then and now, discredit her efforts? On the contrary, it lends a layered complexity to her life and enduring legacy. It forces us to ask questions, engage in debates, and, most importantly, continue the conversation she started. As with any transformative figure, the true worth isn't merely in what is achieved in their lifetime but in the conversations and challenges that continue to unfurl long after they're gone. And in that sense, Amelia's story remains alive — an enduring testament to a life richly lived amidst a whirlwind of controversies and critiques.

The Complexity of Being Amelia

What does it mean to be complex? To be a bundle of contradictions, a tapestry of talents, flaws, and ambitions woven intricately into a single life story? Meet Amelia Bloomer, a woman whose identity extended far beyond the contours of fabric and ink, shaping her into a mosaic of paradoxes that define human complexity.

Amelia wasn't merely born; she erupted into an era begging for seismic shifts. But let's not be fooled. Despite her transformative spirit, she was not an archetype of undiluted rebellion. Born in 1818 in Cortland County, New York, Amelia

Jenks grew up absorbing her times' moral rectitude and social conservatism. Tradition tugged at her sleeves, urging her to fall into the pattern of domestic docility that was practically a woman's birthright. Yet something in her chafed against this predetermined script — was it innate curiosity or intellectual defiance? It's hard to say, but it propelled Amelia into a realm of inquiry and agitation.

The young Amelia could have easily lived her life in the moulds made by society. Her first marriage to David Bloomer — a respectable county official — could have been her golden ticket to societal acceptance. And for a brief chapter, it was. But if you think the matrimony enclosure could stifle Amelia, you're gravely mistaken. Here's where complexity folds in on itself. She was a dedicated wife, yes, but not one to limit her sphere to the hearth. Instead, she transcended traditional marital roles, merging domestic life with uncontainable activism.

Many remember Amelia for the 'Bloomer costume,' a controversial, liberating, and isolating garment. On the surface, what seemed like a simple style choice became a statement that placed Amelia at the crossroads of fashion and activism. The bifurcation wasn't just external; it was internal too. Amelia grappled with the duality of being the trendsetter of a revolutionary attire and the journalist who sought to engage minds, not just alter wardrobes. The bloomers might have granted her fame but also imposed a typecasting she wrestled to shake off.

Ah, the pen — Amelia wielded it like a sword. Her publication, "The Lily," wasn't merely a journal but an ideological battlefield. She fought for temperance and suffrage, exposing her to new influences, like Elizabeth Cady Stanton and Susan B. Anthony. But let's add another layer to her complexity: the dilemmas of allyship. Though part of a vanguard of women's rights, Amelia was not uniformly militant. At times, she was caught between the crosshairs of activists more radical than she was. Was she a moderate being urged to radicalism, or a radical urged to be moderate? The answer is as complex as Amelia herself.

As years advanced, so did her causes. From being at the heart of women's suffrage, Amelia also ventured into the thorny landscape of abolitionism. With each stand came a layer of complexity, adding colours to her already intricate portrait. You see, to be Amelia was to be many things — suffragist, editor, abolitionist, wife, fashion icon, and social pariah. Each role was not an island; they were interconnected, feeding off and contradicting each other.

One could say Amelia was a product of her time. But that would be too simplistic. If anything, Amelia was a dialogue with her times — a conversation fraught with questioning, agreement, tension, and change. As she aged, the fire of activism yielded to embers. Does this mark a regression, a softening of her fiery character, or is it yet another face of her complexity?

While Amelia can't be reduced to a string of labels or confined to a single chapter in history, she encapsulates the complexities inherent in being human. In Amelia's narrative, we find the questions we often ask ourselves: How do we balance tradition and innovation? Conviction and compromise?

Individuality and partnership? And it's precisely in grappling with these questions that we find Amelia's lingering resonance.

The complexity of Amelia Bloomer's life invites us to dissect it and dwell in its nuances, greys, and interlacing contradictions. Herein lies her true legacy — a life not simply lived but fiercely interrogated, a complexity not resolved but embraced. And so, Amelia remains both a question and an answer, an enigma and an open book, a woman as complex as the era she helped to redefine.

Chapter 17

Fading into History

How does one fade into history? It's a paradoxical question. For Amelia Bloomer, a woman who led a life as vibrant as the ink on the pages of The Lily, the notion of 'fading' seems at odds with the dynamism that characterized her existence. Yet here we find ourselves in a chapter that inevitably addresses the waning twilight of her years. It's a time when the public eye tends to look away, preoccupied by the Next Big Thing, the younger champions of causes. But to turn away would be a mistake. For in the stillness of Amelia's later life, the tapestry of her impact continued to weave quietly and persistently.

Amelia Bloomer had been many things — a journalist, an activist, a social reformer. But as years passed, she found herself withdrawing from the front lines. Not from defeat or disinterest but from the realization that battles have seasons, and hers was drawing to a close. The question was — what would she leave behind? What would stay when she no longer could?

In her withdrawal from active campaigning, Amelia, ever the observer, pivoted towards introspection. She engaged in reflective endeavours with the Civil War memory and the suffrage movement gaining momentum without her. Her writings took a meditative turn, shifting from outward advocacy to inward examination. These later works are honest, where Amelia looked back at the complex web she'd spun — a blend of advocacy, personal struggles, and ethical dilemmas. She seemed to be reaching inward, setting the record straight with herself, if not for posterity.

But don't think for a second that Amelia had slipped into obscurity, far from it. She contributed even in her reflective state, still moulding the ongoing dialogue on women's rights. Amelia may have been absent from the podiums and platforms. Still, she had left an indelible mark on the generation that took up the mantle. The women marching toward the victory of the 19th Amendment were fueled, in part, by the winds she had stirred.

Meanwhile, Amelia also took to the simpler joys of life, spending her days in Council Bluffs, Iowa, with her steadfast partner, Dudley. They had moved there from Seneca Falls, a shift reflective of the changing rhythms of their lives. While Dudley involved himself in local journalism, Amelia built a community in this new setting. The couple, side by side, took comfort in a quieter life steeped in mutual respect and shared history.

It was also a period of grief and losses — some public, some deeply personal. Elizabeth Cady Stanton, her friend and a fiery activist, passed away in 1902. The loss was profound but also a stark reminder that the age of their active advocacy was waning. For Amelia and others of her era, the torch was indeed passing.

There's something poetic about Amelia's life coming full circle. The girl who once was hungry for change grew into a woman who instigated it and finally became an elder who could rest, knowing she'd done her part. In a sense, this is the most natural fade into history one can experience. It's not an erasure but a slow retreat, a gentle folding back of oneself into the fabric of a narrative that continues to be written.

Amelia Bloomer faded into history, but only in the way a potent dye fades, never genuinely losing its hue. Even today, her name echoes, her influence reverberates, and her questions continue to be asked. So, did Amelia fade into history? In some ways, yes. But if you look closely, you'll see that what seemed like a fade was a blending of her colours into the larger tapestry of social reform and human rights. And that's a form of immortality few can claim.

Talking about Amelia Bloomer's later years as a 'fading' might be accurate regarding public visibility. Still, I would miss the more nuanced palette of her lifelong contributions. She didn't just fade away; she infused herself into the soil of the causes Amelia nurtured, leaving a legacy that would bloom long after she was gone. And that, dear reader, is not a fade into history. It's a transcendence.

Death and Memorials

A person doesn't just die; they conclude a narrative punctuates a legacy. And so it was with Amelia Bloomer, who exited the world stage on December 30, 1894. But how do you memorialize a woman who was both revolutionary and reflective? What's the epitaph for someone who broke moulds in one moment and then, in the next, retreated into the folds of domestic life?

Amelia Bloomer lived an entire, multifaceted life, and when her time came, it felt like the end of an era. The suffragists who'd once been the young firebrands were ageing. Even as they aged, Amelia's questions remained pertinent through her writings, speeches, and actions. So when she died at her home in Council Bluffs, Iowa, it was more than just the end of an individual; it was the closing of a chapter in the broader story of American social reform.

The obituaries and tributes poured in, some lauding her for her editorial endeavours with "The Lily," others remembering the "bloomer" costume that had caused such a stir. Curiously, the clothing that had garnered ridicule and admiration in equal measure became a focal point in memorials. Why? Because it was a symbol, a shorthand for a life of unapologetic audacity. It's interesting — and perhaps telling — that a piece of attire could carry such weight. Still, then again, Amelia's life was one where symbols often transcended their material forms.

At her funeral, speakers shared anecdotes of her early activism, her lifelong friendships with fellow suffragists like Susan B. Anthony and Elizabeth Cady Stanton, and her enduring partnership with Dudley. Notably, they also acknowledged her later contributions, including her work in Council Bluffs and the impact of her more reflective writings. People realized that Amelia had not so much withdrawn from public life as she had deepened the dimensions of her advocacy.

Now, let's talk about the physical memorials, the plaques, and markers that preserve history. Amelia is honoured in the Seneca Falls National Women's Hall of Fame. This town played host to many of her most formative years. A more traditional granite headstone marks her resting place in Council Bluffs' Fairview Cemetery, featuring a brief but fitting epitaph that reads: "A life dedicated to service and usefulness."

But physical memorials are only a fraction of Amelia Bloomer's sustained influence. As the years turned into decades into a new century, Amelia's legacy was subject to both erosion and revival. A dwindling number of people could claim to have read an issue of The Lily or heard her speak. Yet, Amelia was anything but forgotten. Why? Because the ideas she championed were woven into the fabric of ongoing social conversations. Her essence had dispersed, leaving traces that settled on various platforms, issues, and lives.

It's crucial to understand this: memorials aren't merely about the dead but for the living. And for a woman whose life was a complex interplay of public advocacy and private introspection, the most fitting memorial is this multi-layered influence. Think of Amelia's legacy not just as the plaques or statues but as an ongoing dialogue about women's rights, an ever-relevant discussion around equality, fashion, and individual agency.

Time is a strange thing. In its relentless march, it can dilute memories, even diminish legacies. But some individuals, like Amelia, are so intricately interwoven into the historical fabric that to remove them would unravel the whole tapestry. Amelia Bloomer might not be a household name today, but her imprint is undeniable.

And so, Amelia Bloomer's death becomes not an end but a transition. What started as her foray into social issues has become part of our collective consciousness. For every woman who questioned the status quo, pondered the 'why' behind norms, and pushed the boundaries, Amelia is there — a memorial in spirit, living on in each question asked, each challenge posed, and each small revolution ignited.

Is that not the most poignant of all memorials? A legacy that doesn't just stand still in stone or bronze but one that evolves, resonates, and continues to question long after its originator has passed? That dear reader, is the memorial Amelia Bloomer truly deserves, and, in many ways, it is the one she has.

The Erosion and Revival of Amelia's Legacy

How does one measure the legacy of a life like Amelia Bloomer's? Is it in the stack of yellowed newspapers or perhaps in the faint echoes of speeches delivered on sun-beaten stages? When we talk about Amelia Bloomer's legacy, we grapple with the total of her life's work and its ebb and flow across time. Here lies a woman ahead of her time and, in some ways, ahead of ours. She lived her convictions, sowed seeds of change, and passed on. But what happens to a legacy when the world keeps spinning and time keeps ticking?

In the years immediately following Amelia's death, her legacy seemed to be cementing itself in the cultural lexicon. She remained a known figure in the women's suffrage movement, her work in "The Lily" cited, and her contributions to the Seneca Falls Convention remembered. But as time passed, Amelia's name began overshadowed by others — Elizabeth

Cady Stanton and Susan B. Anthony — women who continued to fight the good fight, extending their activism into the 20th century.

For Amelia, there were no biographies churned out no monuments erected. Despite her tireless efforts, she seemed poised to become a footnote in the history books. Was she, in her way, a victim of her multifaceted nature, the breadth of her activism diluting the potency of her narrative? Could Amelia have fallen into the trap of becoming too nuanced for a world that often demands simple heroes and villains?

In many ways, Amelia Bloomer had faded into the ranks of the "almost famous," her name half-remembered, associated mainly with a style of dress. Academics and scholars mentioned her, but often only in a cursory manner. The world seemed to say, "Yes, we remember Amelia Bloomer, but mainly for her bloomers." Imagine that — a life so rich reduced to a garment.

Then came the waves of feminist scholarship in the mid-20th century, a renewed interest in the suffrage movement, and, more importantly, a growing focus on the multiple dimensions of women's lives. This wave seemed to carry Amelia Bloomer back to the shore of public consciousness. In an era replete with burgeoning discussions on gender roles, sexuality, and public versus private spheres, Amelia once again found herself in sync with the questions of the day. Her complex advocacy — from dress reform to suffrage, journalism to domesticity — was not a liability but an asset for new generations seeking a more nuanced understanding of feminism.

Amelia's writings began to receive renewed attention, not just as historical curiosities but as sophisticated contributions to social and feminist theory. And yes, her name started appearing alongside Stanton's and Anthony's, but not as a secondary figure — rather, as a multifaceted, even radical, pioneer in her own right.

Perhaps most telling has been the inclusion of Amelia Bloomer in educational curricula, marking a revival that assures her story reaches young minds at formative stages. For every schoolchild who learns about Amelia, there is a ripple effect — an understanding that social change can take many forms and that one individual, however overlooked, can make a difference. This educational impact doesn't just renew Amelia's legacy; it breathes new life into it.

Now, we could talk about digital landscapes and social media — modern platforms where Amelia's ideas have found fresh pastures. Indeed, the "bloomer" has even seen a resurgence in fashion circles, especially among women looking for alternatives to the restrictions of contemporary fashion. But to focus solely on these aspects would be reductive. Amelia's true legacy is not in hashtags or trending topics. It lies in the quiet persistence of her ideas, the unending conversations about women's rights, individual freedom, and the complexities of social reform.

Let's remember: legacies aren't static. They fade, sometimes perilously close to oblivion, only to be rediscovered and redefined by new generations. They are not stone monuments but living organisms. Amelia Bloomer's legacy is of this dynamic kind. This legacy declines to be neatly categorized or quietly set aside. And while she may never regain the fame of some of her contemporaries, her influence endures, echoing through the complexities of modern dialogues she seems, almost presciently, to have anticipated.

So here we are, holding the compass of Amelia Bloomer's life, realizing it still points the way. It is as if Amelia Bloomer, ever the trailblazer, has found her way back, not through grand gestures or towering monuments, but through the enduring power of her ideas. Is this not the most enduring of legacies? A conversation that never reasonably concludes, an influence that refuses to wane — this is Amelia Bloomer's true monument.

Chapter 18

Amelia in Modern Discourse

How can history slip into the shadowy corners of collective memory, its figures lingering as vague shapes until someone, or something, brings them back into the light? Isn't it curious how some social reformers gain a permanent place in our textbooks while others fade away? Here, we find Amelia Bloomer — a woman whose audacity and intellect seemed destined to etch her into the annals of American history. Yet, for years, Amelia existed more as a fashion footnote than a pioneering feminist.

Indeed, Amelia Bloomer's legacy had been unfairly eclipsed, often confined to a pair of "bloomers" — an article of clothing she popularized but did not invent. For years, she was a victim of the tendency to trivialize women's contributions by reducing them to what they wore rather than valuing what they did or thought.

But as the 21st century marches on, a resurrection is underway. A new generation of feminists, scholars, and social activists are pulling Amelia back into the limelight. They read her editorials in "The Lily" and admire her friendships with Susan B. Let's talk about her close friendship with Susan B. Anthony and Elizabeth Cady Stanton and her diverse range of activism. Far from being a mere proponent of dress reform, Amelia's voice resounds in modern conversations about gender equality, intersectionality, and social justice.

So, why now? Why has Amelia reentered modern discourse? It's simple: the struggles Amelia was a part of have yet to be fully resolved. Even today, clothing can be a source of judgment against women. Amelia, in her audacity to defy fashion norms, speaks to a new generation confronting body-shaming and rigid gender roles. Her struggle for the right to vote resonates even now, particularly as we grapple with ongoing efforts to disenfranchise voters. Amelia Bloomer is a precursor to today's feminists — advocating for women's education, employment, and autonomy.

The digital age has also played a role in Amelia's revival. Her editorials, once dusty pages in the corners of antiquarian bookstores, are now accessible at the click of a button. Both historians and feminists can dig into Amelia's writings, exploring how she was one of the first female journalists to challenge what society deemed appropriate for women to discuss. Social media campaigns, hashtags, and academic conferences dedicated to Amelia are abundant, offering platforms for her voice to be heard anew.

But Amelia's return to modern discourse is complex. As people pick apart her legacy, they ask how inclusive her feminism was, looking at her views on race and debating whether her methods made a difference. In other words, Amelia Bloomer is no longer a woman confined to a pair of pants or a specific period in history; she's an evolving idea under constant reevaluation.

That's the thing about history — it's not a static, unchanging entity. It is continually rewritten, reframed, and reinterpreted.

Once dimmed by the fog of past years, figures like Amelia can regain their luminosity as society changes and reexamines its values. Amelia popping back up in our modern conversations shows us that history isn't just some dusty old tale; it's a living story that influences who we are today and what we'll become tomorrow. So, as we pull Amelia from the fringes into the core of modern discussions, we also pull her complexities, contradictions, and contributions along with her.

Amelia Bloomer's return to the limelight is more than a revival; it's a reckoning. It speaks to the continual evolution of social discourse and the constant (re)discovery of voices that were never truly silent but were merely waiting for the right moment to be heard. Through Amelia, we realize that the roots of many of our current struggles trace back to the figures who initially dared to stir the pot — figures who remind us that each generation can resurrect forgotten pioneers and make them relevant once more.

Amelia Bloomer may have once been feminism's forgotten foremother, but she is forgotten no longer. The conversations she started long ago echo in our ears today, as persistent and relevant as ever. We look back to her not as a relic but as a beacon — not to tell us where we're going but to remind us how far we've come and how much further we have yet to go.

Feminism's Forgotten Foremother?

In a world teeming with iconic feminists — Elizabeth Cady Stanton, Susan B. Anthony, Sojourner Truth — how can a figure like Amelia Bloomer nearly evaporate from shared memory? Might it be the impermanence of paper, her words printed on the now-yellowed pages of "The Lily"? Or is it the simplistic reduction of her life to a garment — the Bloomer — that swept her under history's rug? In either case, isn't the crucial question: Why have we allowed this vibrant woman to fade into the haze of obscurity?

It seems Amelia found herself on the wrong side of history's selective filter. Her contributions were not less impactful; they were trapped in the gender norms she fought against. For years, her story was suffocated by a corset of misunderstandings. The woman who courageously used her pen and voice to challenge the suffocating social constructs of her time was ironically boxed into the very constraints she aimed to shatter.

The irony doesn't stop there. Amelia was a woman ahead of her time, advocating for suffrage and temperance and identifying the nexus of multiple forms of oppression. Today, we call this intersectionality, but Amelia lived it far before the term was coined. She fought for women's rights to education, jobs, and independence, understanding that true freedom in one aspect of life is incomplete without liberty in the rest. What does it say about our contemporary narratives when this nuanced thinker is reduced to a trouser style?

Let's delve into this a bit more: Amelia Bloomer was more than just a champion for women's rights. She was also a writer with a fire in her belly, a vociferous critic of slavery, and a deep thinker who grappled with life's weighty issues. She didn't just hop onto existing bandwagons — she was instrumental in building them. And yet, we risk allowing her to become feminism's forgotten foremother; her influence slowly washed away like ink on a historical parchment exposed to the elements. Isn't this loss as much ours as it is hers?

Now, there's a tectonic shift. As we recalibrate our moral compasses in the 21st century, we rediscover Amelia. Our current social climate, fraught with dialogue around gender equality and social justice, almost necessitates a reacquaintance with figures like her. Amelia's editorials in "The Lily" could be posted on Medium today. Her friendship with Susan B. Anthony could be a modern-day activist partnership. Her "bloomer costume" might just as quickly trend on social media as a symbol of body positivity and liberation.

The task then falls upon us. Our grappling with questions of equity and justice makes the resurrection of Amelia Bloomer not just important but imperative. She offers us a rearview mirror to see clearly what we're getting right and what we're still struggling with in today's battle for gender equality. Amelia brings the weight of an unfinished revolution, reminding us that although we've come far, the road ahead is still long and winding.

Yet, as she reenters modern dialogue, Amelia is not merely a dusty artefact to be studied but a provocation. She disrupts our comfort zones, questioning our willingness to advocate for change with the same vim that she had. Her life is a mirror, reflecting our advancements and shortcomings.

In lifting Amelia from the pages of history and weaving her back into modern discourse, we're doing more than rescuing a forgotten pioneer. We're inviting an uncomfortable yet vital dialogue about the selective ways we remember our past. So when we ask, "Is Amelia Bloomer feminism's forgotten foremother?" — we're also asking ourselves about the women we might be forgetting now.

Therefore, in resurrecting Amelia, we renewed the pressing issues she addressed. We invite her to sit at the modern table of feminist discourse to both challenge and enrich it. Because, remember, she never really left; we're finally giving her the seat she has always deserved.

The 21st Century Reinterpretation

How do we excavate the essence of a woman like Amelia Bloomer, who lived in a time so different from ours yet faced strikingly similar issues? In the context of today's gender politics, social movements, and fast-paced media, what facets of Amelia's life and work echo in our ears? You see, Amelia isn't simply a historical footnote. She acts like a looking glass, showing us our present-day challenges and victories, helping us see how much progress we've made — and reminding us how much further we still have to go.

Start with social media. Imagine if Amelia had access to Twitter or Instagram. Would she have gone viral to promote the "bloomer costume," or would her thought-provoking editorials in "The Lily" have trended? The hashtags #Bloomer or #TheLily might have been our gateway to her more profound activism, advocacy for women's suffrage, temperance, and commitment to anti-slavery causes. Amelia understood the value of a platform; she harnessed the power of "The Lily" to reach like-minded individuals long before the term "social media influencer" was conceived. In essence, she was ahead of her time, a proto-influencer for issues of dire social importance.

If Amelia were with us today, she would likely be fascinated yet cautious about the double-edged sword of the internet. It would offer her a much larger audience, but would that dilute her message? Would her complex ideas survive the translation into 280 characters or a series of compelling Instagram posts? How would she navigate the virulent criticisms often accompanying outspoken women online? Amelia had a rare gift for nuance; she understood that the issues she fought for were interconnected. Her activism wasn't just about the right to wear pants but about dismantling a system that literally and metaphorically confined women.

Then, consider intersectionality. Amelia was a White woman in a predominantly White movement. Still, she had a deep understanding of the bigger picture when it came to human rights. She would probably have embraced "intersectionality" — a word coined long after her time — better to describe her fight for a world free from oppression. Would Amelia be a voice in the modern movements for gender equality, which now incorporate discussions about race, class, and other social factors? Given her propensity for embracing complex issues, it's highly likely.

And what about the men in Amelia's life, particularly her husband, Dudley? Today's dialogues about supportive partnerships and shared domestic responsibilities echo Amelia's unconventional relationship with her spouse. Dudley was not just her husband; he was her ally, her intellectual companion. Amelia and Dudley offer a prototype of mutual respect and shared advocacy in a society that still wrestles with the concept of a supportive male partner.

When examined through the lens of our modern experience, Amelia's life work offers both a mirror and a window. It reflects the systemic issues we still grapple with and opens vistas into possible possibilities. She was not a woman of half-measures or simplified slogans; she was a woman of action and nuance.

In the 21st century, Amelia Bloomer doesn't just fit neatly into the past; she fits into our questions about the future. She sets a new standard for activism and makes us wonder how we can leave a lasting mark. Today's relevance is not an artefact of her times but a testament to her ideas' enduring power.

So here she is — Amelia Bloomer, not just revisited but reinterpreted, not just remembered but relived. She asks us to admire her for what she was and engage critically with what she represents. If Amelia Bloomer were around today, she'd lead the charge in our societal debates, challenging us to think deeper, act bolder, and strive to be better versions of ourselves. But even in her absence, she occupies that space. After all, isn't that the mark of a true legend? They live on, ever pertinent, ever provoking, challenging each new generation to pick up the mantle and carry on.

Chapter 19

Bloomer's Echo

What's in a name? A lot, especially when the name "Bloomer" rolls off the tongue. But is that name merely a relic of 19th-century fashion or a cornerstone upon which a legacy has been built? Amelia Bloomer, the woman behind the infamous garment and so much more, has left an echo that reverberates. Amelia's life is like an echo because her impact has traveled far, touched numerous things, and returned with fresh levels of meaning.

In the era of the 21st century, where issues of gender equality and women's rights are still points of heated discussion, Amelia's life provides much more than historical fodder. She might have popularized the bloomer costume, which was as revolutionary in fabric as it was in concept. But her impact went much beyond the realm of the sewing machine. The fashion choices of her time, so bounded by societal norms, were not just threads and cloth but a tightly woven tapestry of expectations. Yet Amelia, literally and metaphorically, cut through it — challenging the status quo and liberating herself and others from the constraints of traditional gender roles.

Today's feminists often speak about intersectionality, a word that Amelia might not have known but a concept she deeply understood. Her activism was not a single-issue campaign. Within the ink-stained columns of "The Lily," Amelia wrestled with the pressing issues of her time — calling for women's right to vote, rallying against alcohol abuse, advocating for equal educational opportunities, and vehemently condemning the horrors of slavery. It was as if she sensed that all these strings of injustice were tied together, making the knot even harder to untangle. Amelia's foresight was extraordinary; she intuitively foreshadowed conversations on women's rights and social justice by identifying the interconnectedness of many fights.

I often wonder what Amelia would make of all the viral social justice efforts that use hashtags. Amelia, a pioneer in using media as a tool for activism, would marvel at how messages could now be sent globally instantly. "The Lily" was a slow burn compared to the wildfire speed of today's online movements. The original goal of spreading potentially transformative ideas remained constant. Each retweet or share in today's digital landscape is a modern echo of "The Lily" — an extension of Amelia's conviction that women's voices should be heard.

Then comes the question of recognition — do we remember Amelia Bloomer as we should? Sure, fashion historians will recall her role in the bloomer costume, but does the general populace remember her as a journalistic force and social reformer? Yet, it's hard to ignore that Amelia frequently gets overlooked in the broader women's rights history narrative. Isn't that what happens when history is primarily recorded by those who hold power? Yet, every Women's History Month, every Suffragette celebration, every reference to early feminists brings her back into focus, even if it's a fleeting glimpse. And in those moments, Amelia is neither forgotten nor entirely remembered — she exists in a state of partial remembrance, continually shaping our understanding of what it means to be a woman in America.

What's most intriguing is Amelia's ideology, how her life is continually reinterpreted. A life is so complete and multifaceted that it offers a new lesson each time it's examined. To some, she is the poster child for women's suffrage; to others, a sobering reminder of the incomplete journey towards women's liberation; and to another group, an example of white feminism with its limitations. Amelia Bloomer is not a fixed point but a spectrum of ideas, actions, and interpretations, which explains why she remains relevant.

So, what echo does Amelia Bloomer leave behind in the 21st century? It's not just in the annals of fashion history or the ink of feminist literature. Her echo is in every woman who believes she can bring about change, in every man who supports that change, and in every person who recognizes that social justice is an interconnected web where a tug on one string affects the entire tapestry.

Doesn't that very quality define the essence of a true legend? A powerful echo can have far-reaching effects on culture and philosophy. Amelia Bloomer — a woman, a journalist, an activist, and a pioneer — continues to echo in our lives. And it's an echo that shows no signs of fading.

The Continued Relevance of Amelia Bloomer

How do echoes from the past resonate in our current lives? This isn't a question of mere sentimentality but a pondering the enduring resonance of Amelia Bloomer's life and work. Amelia Bloomer boldly challenged and reshaped conventional social norms, forever marking her place in American history. And yet, here we are, well into the 21st century — a century she'd never see but one that couldn't afford to forget her.

Imagine Amelia, quill in hand, her ink still wet on the pages of The Lily, navigating a tightrope of expectations and societal norms. Her public involvement sparked dialogues of the day and raised poignant questions. Why, for instance, should women abide by clothing conventions that stifled their physical and metaphorical mobility? Amelia understood that clothes were more than fabric; they were statements layered with societal codes and meanings. It's a revelation amid today's discussions about dress rules and the symbolism of our clothing.

Suppose you peruse current feminist literature or social justice courses. In that case, the themes Amelia explored — women's suffrage, temperance, educational rights, and even abolitionism — are all there. But then, Amelia didn't have the vocabulary of "intersectionality" at her disposal. She didn't need it. In her work, there was an innate understanding that all these issues were interlinked — strings in a larger tapestry of systemic oppression. While we may now have more evolved jargon, the substance of the battle remains remarkably similar.

Amelia's lessons extend into the media as well. Remember Amelia's ability to use the media's influence. This tool may either illuminate the truth or muddy people's judgments. Amelia chose illumination. When we glance at today's media landscape, fractured by the diversity of voices yet unified in its global reach, Amelia's foray into journalism serves as a precursor. In our digital age, she would have been captivated by the infectious power of ideas. Were Amelia Bloomer alive today, she'd undoubtedly be a powerhouse in online activism, skillfully using social media as her modern-day pen to ignite change.

And speaking of platforms, what about the physical platforms where women stand today? Women have come far in boardrooms, in the halls of Congress, or on global stages. The fight for fair representation has continued even now. Amelia's struggle for women's equality can teach us about issues that persist in the present. Every woman who casts her vote and breaks a glass ceiling does so atop a foundation built by Amelia and her contemporaries.

Now, there's a tendency to idealize figures like Amelia, to turn them into untouchable icons. But Amelia wasn't a saint; she was a person with limitations. One could argue that her feminism was a product of her time, mostly angled at the liberation of white women. Our adoration for her is matched only by our need to know more, and that's what her narrative has done.

We need a deeper look at feminism that acknowledges its shortcomings while actively striving to expand its circle of supporters.

One might wonder how Amelia herself would perceive her enduring relevance. She might be humbled, possibly even surprised. Yet, deep down, Amelia knew that the issues she was grappling with had a staying power to outlast her life. Her words, choices, and battles made impressions that could not quickly disappear.

So why does Amelia Bloomer matter now? Because she defied simple categorization. Amelia was far more than just a trailblazer in women's fashion or a suffragist fighting for the vote. She had difficulty navigating the nuances of various social concerns, trying to balance grassroots activism and systemic change. Her stories show us the intricacy and depth at the heart of real change, and they challenge us to go beyond the shallow narratives that fit in a tweet.

The resonance of Amelia Bloomer in the present day is not an echo growing fainter but a call that grows ever more loud and clear. It is an invitation to question, disrupt, and strive for a world that loves all of its residents equally. And in that sense, Amelia isn't just a historical figure; she's a contemporary one, her spirit alive in every struggle, victory, and question we have yet to answer.

An Unfading Influence on Women's Lives

Amelia Bloomer — now there's a name etched in the annals of history. But have you ever paused to think about how a woman born over two centuries ago continues to echo in the lives of women today? It's a remarkable tale, filled with the complexities of human challenges and steadfast resilience.

Picture Amelia as a women's rights activist and a person grappling with the human condition. She was raised in 1818 in Cortland County, New York when women's roles were strictly circumscribed. Yet, even as a child, Amelia questioned the hand that fate had dealt her. Her thirst for knowledge set her apart in a world that usually aimed to stifle the intellectual growth of women. For many, questioning the status quo begins with wondering why it exists. And Amelia asked — oh, how she asked.

Fast-forward to Amelia's adult years, a period where destiny met audacity. She moved to Seneca Falls and found her first marriage in shambles. It was a turning point. The breakdown of her initial marriage was not just an ending but a genesis, an awakening. Her second marriage to attorney Dudley Bloomer offered her companionship and an intellectual partnership, a rarity in those times. Many folks are searching for relationships that uplift us, where we feel heard and respected intellectually. Amelia was a trailblazer in that respect, planting the early roots for what we now consider a balanced partnership.

You've probably heard the term "Bloomer costume," but do you grasp the profound act of defiance it represents? Amelia didn't merely change fashion; she changed the narrative. Opting for loose trousers hidden under a skirt wasn't merely a sartorial choice for Amelia; it was her defiant shout against a culture that aimed to limit women in both movement and ambition. Every time we witness women today protesting, running political campaigns, or seizing control of their destinies, we see the living imprint of Amelia's battle for bodily and emotional liberation. Now, let's shift our focus to "The Lily." Amelia wielded her pen to enlighten in a world where media can often be a weapon of mass distortion. Journalism wasn't merely a job for her; it was a calling. Through "The Lily," she argued for temperance and suffrage, fighting a battle against alcoholism and disenfranchisement. Every blog post today that speaks to social justice, every tweet that champions equality, is indebted, in some form, to Amelia's pioneering use of media for activism. Long before the term "disruptor" became a buzzword, Amelia was already shaking things up, using the might of the written word to improve the world around her.

Still, it wasn't a picnic for her either. Amelia faced opposition, whether it was quiet criticism behind closed doors or vehement denunciation from the public. These setbacks do not lessen the fascinating attractiveness of her story but rather strengthen it. Amelia wasn't a static character but a dynamic individual. Amelia faced the thorny issues of her era, be it the struggle against slavery, the turbulence of the Civil War, or the stifling social expectations. Rather than sticking rigidly to her initial opinions, she had the flexibility to evolve her viewpoints. As we work to build a more inclusive world, Amelia's fearless approach to life's obstacles and her willingness to shift her perspective give us enduring wisdom to draw upon.

You might wonder, "What happened to Amelia in her twilight years?" She settled down in Council Bluffs, Iowa, never quite hanging up her advocate's hat — though the volume was somewhat dialed down. The wisdom in her later works, steeped in a life rich with both struggle and victory, resoundingly declares that the role of a change-maker has no expiration date. In a time when we often overlook the insights of older generations, Amelia's lasting impact is a compelling nudge to appreciate the wisdom that frequently matures as we age. So, what makes Amelia's legacy still meaningful to today's women?

Her enduring legacy resembles a richly woven mosaic, constantly shifting and adapting as Amelia did, brimming with fervent convictions and evolving viewpoints. In a time when the pull of social media tempts us to oversimplify complex issues, Amelia's multifaceted legacy warns us not to boil down complicated matters into bite-sized, viral tidbits. Today's women owe her not just for her famous trousers or journalism but for her audacity to question her courage to act and her wisdom to adapt. Amelia may have been a product of the 19th century. Still, she was unmistakably a woman for all seasons — her influence is a tapestry that continues to be woven into the fabric of our lives.

Amelia Bloomer's story isn't just historical; it's instructional. Her life serves as a lens and a guide for modern women navigating complex landscapes. She dared to question, to seek, to act, and yes, even to fail — but she never stopped. Amelia is not merely a woman of her time but a lasting influence. This persistent soul nudges us to wrestle with life's grand dilemmas, brave its hurdles, and stay authentic to who we are. That, my friends, is an influence that refuses to fade.

Chapter 20

Final Thoughts

Who was Amelia Bloomer? Let's pull back the curtain — just a bit — and appreciate the dazzling blend of complexities that made this woman a powerhouse in her time and a lasting symbol beyond it.

When Amelia Bloomer arrived in Seneca Falls in the mid-19th century, she found herself in a community teeming with radical ideas about abolition, temperance, and women's rights. She didn't just adapt to the times; the times adapted to her. What was it about this village, which also harboured the likes of Elizabeth Cady Stanton, that turned it into an incubator for revolutionary thought? Perhaps it was the unique alchemy of personalities or the social upheaval of the period that fused so well with Amelia's sense of urgency.

Bloomer didn't just dip her toes into these issues; she plunged headlong into them. What started as her quiet endorsement of temperance — a social cause that largely marginalized women — evolved into a vocal and relentless call for women's suffrage. Bloomer's most striking transformation was neither planned nor superficial. She wasn't just a woman who popularized a garment that offered physical liberation; she was an intellectual force advocating for the freedom transcending hemlines.

Ah, the Bloomer costume! A loose pair of trousers under a shorter skirt intended to liberate women from the restrictive attire of their time. It is a simple garment, yet its symbolism reverberated for decades. Imagine the audacity it took for Amelia to embrace a fashion that defied conventional norms so radically. Moreover, she used her newspaper, "The Lily," to spread these ideas, allowing fashion to serve as a metaphor for broader societal change. The trousers were not just an item of clothing but an embodiment of rebellion, a scissor-snip at the restricting threads of societal expectations.

Dudley Bloomer, Amelia's husband, was no mere supporting character in her life saga. Their relationship was symbiotic, rooted in a shared quest for social justice. Dudley offered Amelia something exceedingly rare for a woman of her time: a platform and unfettered support for her intellectual and moral pursuits. This wasn't a mere marital alliance but a partnership challenging the status quo. How many husbands of that period would have had the vision — or the courage — to support their wives in such endeavours wholeheartedly?

As Amelia aged, her influence expanded. Now, one would expect the fire to simmer down. But not Amelia. The turn of the century saw her move to Council Bluffs, Iowa, where she continued challenging and rebuilding communities. Even as the women's suffrage movement fractured into various factions, Amelia remained a steady voice for unity and progress. Her later writings served as social commentaries and wisdom-laden letters to future generations.

Her life was not without its challenges and criticisms. No life committed to radical change could be. There were controversies and moments when Amelia faced opposition from conservative onlookers and fellow reformers. Yet, even in moments of doubt, she stayed committed to her core principles. There was no retiring from a life devoted to justice and equality; the fire of her early years in Seneca Falls never dwindled but morphed into a steady, enduring glow.

Amelia Bloomer's legacy differs from one that can be neatly packaged into digestible bits of historical trivia. It is threaded through the very fabric of the women's rights movement, the struggle for equal rights, and the conversations around social reform that we still have today. Do her contributions still matter? Absolutely. The tapestry of Amelia Bloomer's life serves as both a mirror and a window — reflecting the strides made and revealing the lengths yet to go in the unfinished revolution for women's equality.

We might say Amelia Bloomer was ahead of her time, but that would be doing her a disservice. She was precise about her time, and the world needed to catch up. And in pondering the continued relevance of this remarkable woman, we find that we're still catching up. What could be more enduring than that?

The Bloomer Legacy: An Unfinished Revolution

So, what does it mean to launch an unfinished revolution? Is it a mark of failure or an indication of everlasting influence? When it comes to Amelia Bloomer, the term "unfinished revolution" is less about what she couldn't complete and more about what she set in motion.

Born in 1818 in Homer, New York, Amelia was out of sync with her times, or perhaps it was the era that wasn't entirely aligned with women like Amelia. The youngest of six, Bloomer embodied the whispers of change that a new century carried on its wind. This was a woman who didn't just follow the cultural scripts laid before her. Instead, she crumbled them up, penning her lines in ink that would last through centuries.

In the formal sense, education wasn't abundant for Amelia — a narrative familiar to many women of her epoch. But let us not confuse schooling with education. This woman was self-taught, reading anything she could get her hands on, proving that diplomas don't satiate intellectual hunger. When she moved to Seneca Falls in 1840, it was as if a spark met tinder. She dived into the intellectual ferment of the time, rubbing shoulders with the likes of Elizabeth Cady Stanton.

Now, revolutionaries aren't born; they're made. Amelia Bloomer was no exception. Married at 22 to attorney Dudley Bloomer, it was as if destiny was aligning the stars for both of them. Dudley was an editor who believed in the potency of the written word, and he introduced Amelia to the power of the press. Can we underestimate the profound impact this must have had on a woman so full of thoughts and itching for an outlet?

And then came "The Lily." Originally a temperance journal, under Amelia's nurturing, it transformed into something much larger — a platform advocating not just temperance but women's suffrage and rights. What initially began as a small newsletter bloomed into a force that couldn't be ignored. This newspaper became Amelia's weapon, her way of reaching into the homes of American women and encouraging them to question, demand, and act.

Who needs to remember the Bloomer costume? A fashion statement, yes, but also a manifest declaration of independence. Trousers beneath a short skirt — a deceptively simple design that unleashed complex discussions. The Bloomer attire was far more than a controversial fashion choice; it was an emblem of defiance against societal norms, a walking representation of freedom. Amelia knew the potency of symbols, and this one resonated deeply. It might have drawn mockery but also drew attention, sparking long overdue dialogues.

Amelia wasn't a solitary figure in the women's rights movement. Alongside Elizabeth Cady Stanton and Susan B. Anthony, she formed part of an intellectual triumvirate that profoundly influenced each other. Yet, it wasn't just ideas she shared but camaraderie, challenges, and triumphs. Their friendships were with disagreements and complex dynamics. Could friendships that carry the weight of a revolution be anything but intricate?

Amelia Bloomer's life was more than the sum of her public deeds. This woman struggled and triumphed, facing opposition from society and, at times, from within her circle of reformers. Controversy seemed to follow her, but when has a revolution ever been uncontroversial? The measure of her courage lies not just in her accomplishments but also in her resilience to carry on despite setbacks.

It's been over a century since Amelia Bloomer passed away. Yet, her voice resonates in today's dialogues around women's rights, voting rights, and social reforms. Is this not the definition of an unfinished revolution? A revolution not confined by the limitations of time or space, one that encourages new generations to pick up the torch she once held.

When we talk about Amelia's legacy, it's tempting to catalogue it — suffrage, journalism, fashion — but to do so would diminish the indomitable spirit she symbolized. Amelia Bloomer was neither the beginning nor the end of the fight for women's rights; she was a crucial chapter in a written tale. She handed us not a completed manuscript but a pen, inviting us to continue sketching out the ever-evolving landscape of human rights. How's that for an unfinished revolution?

The Tapestry of Amelia Bloomer's Contributions

What shapes a life that bends the arc of history? Is it innate brilliance, fortuitous circumstance, or perhaps an unyielding spirit? When we unravel the intricate tapestry of Amelia Bloomer's life, each thread tells a tale of courage, innovation, and resilience.

Born Amelia Jenks in 1818 in upstate New York, Bloomer entered a world with preconceived notions about what a woman's life should look like. The youngest of six siblings, Amelia grew up with limited formal schooling but an insatiable curiosity. Her education wasn't a product of classrooms; it arose from the simple yet profound act of reading. The young Amelia consumed literature, philosophy, and current events as if she were starved for them. The lack of a formal diploma hardly contained her intellectual hunger. Who could have guessed this thirst would catalyze seismic changes in American society?

At age 22, Amelia married Dudley Bloomer, an attorney and newspaper editor. She married into the role of a traditional housewife. Still, Amelia didn't believe in being confined to pre-determined roles. Dudley introduced Amelia to the editorial world, a match that proved electric. Can you imagine the vitality she felt, wielding a pen as a sword for the first time? It's like giving a master musician their first instrument, right?

Her first foray into publishing came through her husband's newspaper. Still, soon, Amelia felt the pull to create a platform. Enter "The Lily," a periodic that initially focused on temperance but would soon expand its scope to become a clarion call for women's rights. Yes, the world had publications, but none spoke so directly to the women of that era as did Amelia's paper. It challenged its female readers to question societal roles, reevaluate their aspirations, and arm themselves with knowledge and confidence. In those pages, Bloomer not only discussed matters of suffrage and equality but also dared to touch upon controversial issues like marital laws and women's financial independence. This wasn't just journalism; it was a rallying cry.

Then came the Bloomer costume — trousers paired with a short skirt. It might appear a mere stylistic statement today but in the 1850s? It was an act of rebellion. Adopted from the original design of Elizabeth Smith Miller, the costume struck the heart of Victorian norms. And Amelia, through her platform, became its most vocal advocate. This piece of clothing wasn't just fabric and thread; it was a manifestation of the yearning for personal and public space women desperately sought. Fashion is often dismissed as frivolous, but what if it's another language through which revolutions can be whispered?

Amelia's contributions to women's rights weren't enacted in isolation. She was part of a more extraordinary tapestry of feminist reformers — individuals like Elizabeth Cady Stanton and Susan B. Anthony. Together, they were more than just friends; they were co-conspirators in the best sense of the term. Yet, friendships in revolutionary settings are seldom without strain. While Amelia found herself at odds with some of Stanton's and Anthony's more radical proposals, she never let these disagreements undermine their collective goals. That takes a certain wisdom.

Bloomer's tapestry of contributions extended beyond women's rights. She advocated for temperance, understanding the corrosive effects of alcohol, particularly on women and children in a society that offered them little legal protection. It was a view often overshadowed by her feminist activities but integral to her holistic approach to social reform.

But what distinguishes Amelia's legacy? Is it the publication of "The Lily"? Is it her pioneering role in fashion as a form of protest? Or it could be her uncanny ability to stir public discussion and act as a conduit for collective change. Amelia Bloomer didn't just contribute one thread to the tapestry of women's rights; she wove an entire section, integrating media, fashion, and social activism themes. Her work wasn't limited to a single domain; instead, it straddled multiple spheres, weaving them into a coherent narrative of emancipation. That's the essence of her unfinished revolution.

By passing in 1894, Amelia had laid the groundwork for seismic shifts in public thought and policy. But revolutions don't conclude; they evolve. Amelia handed us a tapestry still in the making. She gave us a narrative that beckons us to keep the loom busy, to add our threads to the ones already intricately laid down. And so, the tapestry of Amelia Bloomer's contributions remains unfurled, inviting us to examine it, learn from it, and, most importantly, to continue weaving.

Notes and References

When we try to pierce the veils of time and sift through the pages of history, we rely on many sources — primary documents, firsthand accounts, newspapers, etc. One could even argue that the very texture of biography is spun from the threads of these invaluable references. After all, how else can we genuinely fathom the intricacies of Amelia Bloomer's life and contributions?

The cornerstone of understanding Bloomer's journey starts with "The Lily." It was not merely a newspaper but a groundbreaking platform through which Bloomer articulated her arguments for women's rights and temperance. You'd need to dive into its archives to find the story's heart. Old editions have been preserved and are accessible through multiple educational institutions. Delving into those pages is akin to conversing with Amelia herself — each word echoing her thoughts, each article a window into her revolutionary ideals.

We also rely heavily on Amelia's correspondence with her contemporaries, Elizabeth Cady Stanton and Susan B. Anthony. In these letters, you don't just get the reformer or the journalist; you get the woman — her aspirations, apprehensions, and quirks. The Elizabeth Cady Stanton & Susan B. Anthony Papers Project offers a treasure trove of this correspondence. Letters weren't just ink on paper for these women; they were a lifeline connecting them and the cause they fervently espoused.

Biographies that have come before also provide a contextual framework. One standout is "Amelia Bloomer: A Biography" by Kathleen Bowman, a comprehensive account that delves into the historical, social, and political elements that influenced and were influenced by Bloomer. It fills in the gaps, providing what might be considered the 'flesh and bones' to the 'soul' you find in primary sources like letters and newspaper articles.

Similarly, academic articles often give us a microscopic view of Amelia's life. These are not just dry, factual accounts. Think of them as close-up shots in a film that bring you face-to-face with pivotal moments. Articles like "The Evolution of "The Lily" and the Changing Voice of Amelia Bloomer" by Patricia Marks give a more nuanced insight into how her ideas and vocalizations evolved.

Take into account historical context. Texts that provide background into the women's suffrage movement, temperance, and 19th-century America offer a stage upon which Amelia's actions can be more deeply understood. Recommended readings include "The Road to Seneca Falls" by Judith Wellman and "Women and Temperance" by Ian Tyrrell. Remember, Amelia Bloomer didn't operate in a vacuum. Knowing the landscape of her time adds depth and colour to the tapestry of her life.

The weaving of this biographical narrative was only complete with an acknowledgement of the digital age. Databases such as JSTOR and the American Memory Project by the Library of Congress have made gathering historical texts and correspondences a task that can be done without leaving one's desk. This convenience should respect the integrity and impact of these original documents. Indeed, these platforms act as the guardians of history, keeping the essence of Amelia's legacy alive for new generations to discover.

So, when you turn the pages of this biography, know that each sentence is the culmination of a myriad of sources, each carefully selected and pondered upon. The notes and references aren't just the scaffolding; they are as much a part of Amelia Bloomer's story as the words you've read. Just as Amelia stood on the shoulders of the women who came before her, this narrative stands on the robust foundations of meticulous research and historical reverence. And in that way, Amelia Bloomer continues to live on — not just in the story told but also in the story yet to be discovered.

Made in the USA
Las Vegas, NV
01 December 2023

81914810R00118